INNOVATION FROM WITHIN

INNOVATION FROM WITHIN

REDEFINING HOW NONPROFITS SOLVE PROBLEMS

Stephanie Cosner Berzin
AND
Humberto Camarena

OXFORD
UNIVERSITY PRESS

OXFORD

UNIVERSITY PRESS

Oxford University Press is a department of the University of Oxford. It furthers
the University's objective of excellence in research, scholarship, and education
by publishing worldwide. Oxford is a registered trade mark of Oxford University
Press in the UK and certain other countries.

Published in the United States of America by Oxford University Press
198 Madison Avenue, New York, NY 10016, United States of America.

© Oxford University Press 2018

Library of Congress Cataloging-in-Publication Data
Names: Cosner Berzin, Stephanie, author. | Camarena, Humberto, author.
Title: Innovation from within : redefining how nonprofits solve problems /
Stephanie Cosner Berzin and Humberto Camarena.
Description: New York : Oxford University Press, 2018. |
Includes bibliographical references and index.
Identifiers: LCCN 2017042786 (print) | LCCN 2017058968 (ebook) |
ISBN 9780190858803 (updf) | ISBN 9780190858810 (epub) |
ISBN 9780190858797 (paperback)
Subjects: LCSH: Technological innovations—Management. | Problem solving. |
Nonprofit organizations—Management.
Classification: LCC HD45 (ebook) | LCC HD45 .C684 2018 (print) |
DDC 658.4/063—dc23
LC record available at https://lccn.loc.gov/2017042786

CONTENTS

PART III   INNOVATION FOR THE FUTURE

ABOUT THE AUTHORS

Stephanie Cosner Berzin, PhD, is Assistant Dean, Doctoral Program and an Associate Professor at the Boston College School of Social Work. As co-founder of the Social Innovation + Leadership Program, Dr. Berzin co-led the curriculum redesign and development of the strategic vision for social innovation at the school. Dr. Berzin serves as Co-Director of the Center for Social Innovation, where she conducts research and supports organizational capacity-building around innovation and intrapreneurship. Her research and consulting work with hundreds of social sector leaders supports the development of an innovation skill set and helps build organizational capacity for change. As the principal investigator on more than 20 projects related to social intrapreneurship and author of more than 50 publications, her work promotes the capacity of existing agencies to respond to social issues.

Humberto Camarena, MSW, is an Adjunct Professor and Administrator at the Pontificia Universidad Católica de Chile School of Social Work where he teaches social innovation and develops social impact projects with government, nonprofit, and for-profit organizations. Prior to this, he was the Assistant Director of the Boston College Center for Social Innovation and directed the implementation of multiple interorganizational social innovation labs in Latin America. Humberto's work through innovation collaboratives has generated social impact in diverse issues including peace and conflict resolution, education, housing and homelessness, environmental sustainability, and women's entrepreneurship.

INTRODUCTION

Social innovation, social entrepreneurship, social enterprise, design thinking, social impact bonds, b-corps, crowdfunding, impact investing, social intrapreneurship—these words represent a host of new strategies to approaching today's most pressing problems. After decades of hard work, nonprofits continue to address a multitude of significant social challenges, and social innovation provides hope that new frameworks and strategies will get us closer to creating groundbreaking sustainable solutions. Our work with hundreds of nonprofit leaders over the past 10 years reminds us again and again that nonprofit organizations can and must play a leading role in developing and implementing these solutions. But doing so takes retooling, rethinking, and reenergizing ourselves toward innovation.

The nonprofit sector has seen more diversity and change in the past 25 years than ever before. There is huge growth in the sector and interest from across sectors in finding new solutions to social problems. There are new strategies being used to support social need and new players engaged in problem-solving. The nonprofit sector stands at a time of unprecedented change, and the sector must respond to be ready for these shifts. Nonprofit leaders must take leadership in driving transformation and cultivating the social sector of tomorrow. Existing nonprofit leaders must engage in this new landscape, maintain their role in this dialogue, emphasize their expertise in the social context, and leverage their relationships with the community to drive the new narrative for the future. By leading this dialogue, the nonprofit field's commitment to social justice and equity can permeate thinking about innovation.

One nonprofit leader in a recent study we conducted said the following about engaging in innovation: "Either we do this or think about doing something else, because if we stand still, we will get run over." This is today's reality, and nonprofit leaders need to be prepared. *Innovation from within* is about preparing the field for this context by redefining how we think about innovation and providing practical tools to make this leap.

In our current context, there are interconnected, complex social problems; increased competition for scarce resources; and social, political, and economic conditions that impact giving. These are times when emergent health crises, environmental catastrophes, and huge strains on social services create challenges for our sector. But this time period also includes tremendous technological advances, gains in knowledge and resources, more partners and players engaging in social solutions, and more opportunities to leverage what we know. This time period creates the opportunity for the nonprofit sector to capitalize on its history of solving problems, engaging with the community, creating successful partnerships, and actively understanding social need. But this can only be done if we build on these successes and opportunities through the lens of social innovation.

Innovation has always been an inherent part of the sector. It has always pushed nonprofits toward new methods of problem-solving and new programs and services to more efficiently and effectively address need. Today, however, innovation means even more than new solutions: it is a transformational mindset and an active *process* that can be taught and can be encouraged. Innovation is about building capabilities and processes that enable new ideas to emerge. Hill, Brandeau, Truelove, and Lineback (2015) discuss three capabilities of innovation: creative abrasion, creative resolution, and creative agility. This three-part structure of collaborative problem-solving, integrative decision-making, and experimentation, respectively, provides one lens into how innovation capacity is developed. Nonprofits need to find their own brand of innovation that celebrates their distinct competencies and capacities.

The current environment does celebrate innovation in the sector. Nationally and globally, new programs, products, and services have been developed to solve social problems ranging from health to water access to education to poverty. These examples (see the box "Examples from the Field") are astounding in terms of scope, innovation, and impact. But they almost exclusively speak to the development of *new* products and *new* organizations designed to respond to social needs. They highlight entrepreneurs who saw a problem and developed a new process, policy, product, or program to respond. They capture heroes who solve social problems; heroes who emerged sometimes from within the field of their work and sometimes with little experience in the particular issue prior to their project. But current dialogue about social innovation fails to capture the enormous contributions and potential of *innovation from within*.

Examples from the Field

Embrace Warmer brings simple, clean, effective temperature stabilization to newborn babies to fight hypothermia (http://www.embraceglobal.org)

Delancy Street Foundation was founded as a residential education center for substance abusers, ex-convicts, and homeless individuals to get help through training and social enterprise (http://www.delanceystreetfoundation.org/)

Water.org forms community partnerships to develop water and sanitation projects that brings clean water to all (http://water.org/)

Plumpy'Nut was developed to bring low-cost, ready-to-use nutrition to combat childhood malnutrition (http://www.edesiaglobal.org/)

SpritHorse International supports children with disabilities through equine therapy (http://www.spirithorsetherapy.com/)

More Than Words uses a social enterprise model to empower youth who are in foster care, court-involved, homeless, or out of school (http://mtwyouth.org/)

WHY WE NEED *INNOVATION FROM WITHIN*

These projects—and the majority of media attention—fail to capture or acknowledge the tremendous innovation activities and innovation potential of *existing* nonprofits. What they do not highlight are the innovations occurring *within* nonprofits that do not lead to new organizations. And they do not highlight the pathway by which these innovations occurred. They focus on the tireless entrepreneur who emerged to solve a challenging problem and did it with determination, ingenuity, and impact. But innovation doesn't have to come solely from an individual, heroic entrepreneur with an outstanding idea. What if innovation could be harnessed? What if the assets, skills, and resources of existing organizations could be utilized in new ways to unleash even more examples of social innovation? What if the heroes who *already* work with the populations they want to support and who *already* know a lot about the complex problems they wish to solve can be transformed into *intrapreneurs*? What if nonprofit organizations can build or enhance their innovation capacity to develop, generate, and implement innovation? Our work with nonprofit leaders has convinced us that this is possible.

We have used different models of nonprofit engagement including traditional training, the Social Innovation Lab (a capacity-building and leadership design-thinking initiative), an innovation incubator, and a challenge competition to incite, breed, develop, implement, and sustain social innovations in eight countries. Agency partners have tackled diverse problems including youth violence, air pollution, homelessness, Alzheimer's disease, education, fundraising, staff relationships, incarceration, urban renewal, and foster care. Through this work, we have learned three critical things:

1. Nonprofits can successfully engage in the development, implementation, and sustainability of innovation given the right resources and supports.
2. Nonprofits bring distinct assets and resources to innovation work, including skills, expertise, commitment, infrastructure, and existing relationships with beneficiaries, communities, government, and private industry.
3. Innovation within existing nonprofits brings solutions to scale.

Existing nonprofits have survived through the ups and downs of economic hardship and weathered great social challenges. They have responded in multiple situations and with both individuals and communities over time. They have built infrastructures that can get solutions to many people across diverse communities. If we could harness this energy and their resources, then social innovation can reach its true potential. Then we can understand the potential impact of *innovation from within*.

While nonprofit leaders may acknowledge the need to engage in innovation work, many existing social sector leaders have not been trained with this perspective. They have been trained for management, for direct service, for policy advocacy, and for community building. They have been trained to understand complex social issues and to work deeply within communities. By building on these attributes, innovation competencies can be developed. Innovation tools can be integrated into the nonprofit workplace, and 21st-century skills for innovation can be fostered among current and future staff. Existing social sector leaders can learn how to initiate a culture of innovation, develop and define innovation challenges, create innovation solutions, and integrate innovation into their mandate. They can build on their capacity and capitalize on existing strengths to fight the world's toughest problems.

To build the capacity for innovation requires attention to building organizations and individuals who are ready and have the right tools to develop, implement, and sustain innovations. *Innovation from within* provides a framework specific for nonprofits through the Nonprofit Innovation Model (IN Model). The IN Model guides leaders in developing and implementing *innovation from within* their own nonprofit organization. The time has come to get more people into the business of solving problems in extraordinary ways and to amplify the impact of the field of social innovation by bringing along the people who provide the bulk of services and impact. This book is both the guide and a call to action for building that momentum.

HOW TO USE *INNOVATION FROM WITHIN*

This book has been designed for changing practice and creating new dialogue. It can be used for reorienting, retraining, and inspiring staff. It can be used in its entirety, as a handbook for a specific project, or in pieces for activities and ideation. It can be used to remake an organization, to support new leadership practices, or to provide education to support the nonprofit sector of tomorrow. This book is meant to outline the social innovation environment and set the stage for innovation work within existing nonprofit agencies.

This book is divided into three distinct parts to provide readers with an opportunity to think about the context of and concepts around social innovation before getting into the work. Part I is about redefining social innovation for the nonprofit context, and challenging our individual perspectives on what innovation is and who should practice it. Part II is about *action* in the context of organizations. Part III is about changing the nonprofit sector.

Part I, Innovation Redefined, outlines why we need innovation and provides the language for nonprofit leaders to operate in this context. Chapter 1 sets the stage for innovation by outlining key concepts and multiple pathways to innovation. Chapter 2 conceptualizes innovation in the nonprofit context, with its unique opportunities and challenges, and outlines the IN Model, a process to support innovation work for nonprofits. In Chapter 3, we explore the right conditions for innovation work, looking at people, tools, and the mindset necessary for successful innovation.

Part II of the book shifts to Innovation in Action. We use the IN Model to support agencies to develop innovation not once, but over and over again. These activities can be used to fuel an entire process of innovation at the agency or as individual exercises for innovation. The IN Model is organized into four phases to stimulate, develop, implement, infuse, and sustain innovation. Chapter 4, *Initiate,* helps build the right agency culture, climate, and personnel for innovation. Chapter 5, *Investigate,* provides strategies for defining the problem you set out to solve and collecting meaningful information from the communities you intend you work with. Chapter 6, *Innovate,* is about developing and testing innovative solutions. Chapter 7, *Integrate,* prepares you to implement and scale the innovation, evaluate for social impact, and integrate innovation back into your organization and sector. In each phase, strategies and tools are provided that not only discuss what needs to happen, but that also give you the activities to accomplish this. Part II provides tools to support developing, implementing, sustaining, and integrating innovation.

The final section gazes toward the future, one in which innovation becomes part of the core DNA of the sector. Part III moves beyond innovation at the individual organizational level and asks the reader to consider what will be required to make innovation central to the nonprofit field. Chapter 8 illuminates three critical factors for sectorial change; resources, a role in defining innovation, and developing the next generation of leaders. Chapter 9 closes the book by integrating the lessons from all three parts of the book. It emphasizes the imperative of nonprofit engagement in innovation and the benefits of this participation for responding to social problems.

This book stimulates innovation work in existing organizations. It provides conceptual frameworks, background and definition, and concrete steps for action. It is about creating innovators and vitalizing innovative organizations by expanding their vision and providing the tools to act. It is about emphasizing the importance of nonprofits in inspiring and implementing innovation. It is about understanding problems, generating solutions, and developing sustainable innovation.

Becoming an innovative organization and seeding innovation in the nonprofit sector is not just about doing one innovative project. It is not about developing a product or a new service in isolation. It is about doing innovation over and over. It's about having the structure, support, and enthusiasm to fluidly respond to new challenges with new solutions. It is about creating an individual, organizational, and sectorial culture that understands innovation and sees the innovation imperative. Diana Aviv, President and CEO Independent Sector, said

> Imagine a sector driven by leaders who govern organizations capable of pivoting adroitly in the face of complexity. Imagine leaders who see in failure a chance to learn and prosper. Imagine leaders who share a vision across fields of practice, forge networks to tackle ballooning social problems, and cultivate an entrepreneurial environment throughout the social sector. Imagine the high caliber of a workforce that reflects the rainbow of diversity across America, and in doing so, becomes more innovative than ever. (Hansen-Turton & Torres 2014)

This is the nonprofit sector of the future, one that understands and demands innovation and leads social problem-solving from within. It is about unleashing the creativity and assets of existing organizations and using them to complement the entrepreneurial pathways to innovation. Nonprofits need strategies and tools to make this happen. *Innovation from within* begins to provide these tools and build the momentum for the sector.

INNOVATION FROM WITHIN

PART I

INNOVATION REDEFINED

Social innovation is about finding better, more effective, more efficient solutions to social problems. As individuals committed to positive impact, we look to use every available tool to drive social justice. This book is designed to contribute unconventional tools and thinking by exploring innovation and its use in the nonprofit community. Part I is designed to examine definitions and concepts of social innovation. As much of the innovation lexicon has developed outside of the existing nonprofit community, new dialogue can engage broader participation and create accessibility for nonprofit professionals. In this section of the book, we ask you to consider the nonprofit role in innovation and to delve into what it takes to purposefully build for innovation. In Part I, we ask you, the individual, to engage, to reflect, and to question. Part I sees individual engagement as the platform to establish innovation in organizations and to support innovation in the sector.

Chapter 1 begins by challenging you to consider and perhaps recalibrate your current understanding of social innovation. Definitions of social innovation vary tremendously with less clarity around related concepts (i.e., social entrepreneurship, social intrapreneurship, social enterprise, social ventures, etc.). Speaking the same language enhances our ability to engage in innovation conversations and creates an environment for collaboration. In this chapter, we present an inclusive framework for innovation outcomes that goes beyond the solution as a new organization, product, or program. We ask you to consider the potential impact of disrupting traditional paradigms or changing structure and process. Entrepreneurship and intrapreneurship are presented as complementary paths to innovation. Through this chapter, we ask you to consider social innovation as a process. You will be pushed to broaden current conceptualizations of innovation to be inclusive of multiple pathways and solutions, and to consider social innovation not only as an outcome, but as an iterative process that can and should be applied within nonprofits.

While rethinking innovation is an important step, nonprofits have a long history of developing new solutions and transforming responses to meet social need. Chapter 2 builds on that history and asks how nonprofit organizations can leverage assets to support innovation work. Some nonprofit leaders may be hesitant, or less convinced of their need or ability to innovate; barriers related to resources certainly play a role. This chapter asks nonprofits to consider not only why innovation work supports their ability to make impact, but also how innovation can benefit from nonprofit engagement. While it may be appealing to consider innovation as the domain of the lone inventor, that would limit our ability to leverage the assets, capacity, good ideas, relationships, and human, financial, and social capital of existing organizations. The Nonprofit Innovation Model is introduced as a design thinking oriented approach that acknowledges those assets and the challenges that come from doing innovation as an intrapreneur in the nonprofit context.

After establishing the potential for expanding innovation work in the sector, chapter 3 discusses how to build an organization for innovation. Innovative agencies are made, not born; they are purposefully built with resources, structures, and processes. Building for innovation requires developing the right human capital, adopting specific tools, and expanding the mindset to be open and ready for this work. Chapter 3 looks to catalyze change in organizations by preparing individuals to know what it takes to create an innovative agency. In the nonprofit context, innovation requires consideration and planning. It may involve shifting resources, developing capacity, and (re)aligning priorities. Developing innovation ambassadors promotes the likelihood for this to occur.

Throughout Part I, you are asked to consider and reflect on innovation and its use in the nonprofit sector. It can be used to stimulate dialogue about definitions and expand discussions across discipline. It can be used to prepare you for Part II to unleash innovation in your organization and engage in the activities of the Nonprofit Innovation Model. The content can also be used to help you champion innovation in the sector as outlined in Part III. While organizational and sectoral level change are important to *innovation from within*, it all stems from the work of the individual, so let's get started.

REFRAME SOCIAL INNOVATION

Chapter 1 introduces concepts for social innovation that support a broader conceptualization and an inclusive framework.

Get ready to ...

1. Acquire a new language for social innovation.
2. Structure innovation in terms of conceptual frameworks, pathways, and outcomes.
3. Open your mind to new solutions for social change.

Recently, everyone has hopped on the social innovation bandwagon. It has become a call to many to "fix" broken systems and to solve the world's challenges with radical solutions. It has motivated career changers and encouraged unlikely suspects to engage in transformative social action. We see the term popping up in media, foundations, organizations, and even government. But, truthfully, if we think about it, early reform workers have always promoted innovation in the social sector. Factory protections, social security, the women's rights movement, public health programs, universal education, services and support for the poor, and child welfare protections are examples of social innovations that have historically changed our response to social problems. So, what is different about today's social innovation discussions? Why do we need to consider social innovation? Why is it critical to be a part of writing these definitions?

Dialogue about social innovation today provides the opportunity for a different set of discussions—discussions that broaden the definition of innovation and include a range of players, create the possibility for new resources, and open up the reach of solutions. But rather than entering the innovation space and accepting current definitions, nonprofits must challenge and reconsider these meanings. This allows us to consider multiple outcomes as equally important and multiple pathways as equally viable. It allows us to contextualize innovation space so that it is relevant to nonprofits and centers social justice values as a core part of innovation work. This chapter provides the background to begin engaging in these discussions.

DEFINITIONS OF SOCIAL INNOVATION: BUZZWORD OR FIELD CHANGE?

There has been pervasive dialogue around social innovation across sectors. We see an innovation undercurrent in the way each sector talks about the future and the ability to make change. And, in the social sector, we see a focus on social innovation as a potential panacea for solving the world's most complex problems. But nonprofits have always made quality improvements and worked to make continual advances to address social problems. They have a history of testing and piloting interventions that eventually become the gold standard of care. So, what is new about social innovation? Is this just another buzzword or new jargon that speaks to the way work has always been done?

While working to improve practice and ameliorate social problems is certainly not new, "social innovation" as a term and a formalized process *is* new and represents an opportunity to change the field. It is a movement that brings new tools to the process of problem-solving, brings new players to addressing social need, and opens the range of solutions that may be considered. It expands our thinking so that solutions may be programmatic or service-oriented, but they may also involve technological advances or enterprise structures. It blurs the nonprofit and for-profit boundaries and expands our thinking about what structures can be used to address social issues. Social innovation asks for new collaborators or partnerships, and it fundamentally transforms how we think about addressing social problems. It is these new tools and methodologies, these new partnerships and collaborations, this new use of knowledge and technological advances, and this new openness to a wider range of solutions that creates the opportunity for true field change.

For many, social innovation can be thought of as an umbrella term that encompasses our growing vocabulary of how we can transform the way we respond to and solve social problems. Different from the kind of innovation that refers to a process, method, product, or outcome that is new and creates any improvement, *social innovation* speaks explicitly to the solution of a social problem. Most definitions emphasize social innovation outcomes and the development of more effective, more efficient solutions to social problems (Phills, Deiglmeier, & Miller 2008). Phills, Deiglmeier, & Miller (2008, p. 36) defined social innovation as, "a novel solution to a social problem that is more effective, efficient, sustainable, or just than existing solutions and for which the value created accrues primarily to society as a whole rather than private individuals" Social innovations not only respond to the presenting problem but also enhance society's ability to act (Murray, Caulier-Grice, & Mulgan 2010). Other definitions highlight the importance of collaborative or social relationships to solutions, the inclusion of technological or digital advances, and contributions to systems change (Rüede1 & Lurtz 2012). Each definition focuses on a slightly different topic but shares the common theme of transformational response to social problems. Definitions often highlight the outcomes achieved, with a tendency to claim innovation only after it has occurred.

From our work with nonprofit agencies, it is clear that social innovation is more than just the outcomes that we recognize after the fact. Social innovation can go beyond just this solution approach and also be thought of as the processes or practices that lead to these innovative solutions. Social innovation encompasses a focus on both process and outcome:

> Social innovation is an umbrella term that encompasses multiple pathways and processes that address the root causes of social injustices. The solutions are more effective, efficient, and/or sustainable—socially, economically, and environmentally—than previous solutions and are a result of collaboration with diverse stakeholders.

Newer definitions need to consider not only outcomes, but also the processes used to achieve them. *The Open Book of Social Innovation* (Murray et al. 2010) documents this work, sharing methods and tools for innovating across sectors. It provides strategies for inspiring innovation, developing and testing solutions, and implementing and scaling solutions. It is a starting point, but innovating from within existing nonprofits requires new methods and approaches to support the work that recognize the unique strengths and challenges of launching innovations from within. In our recent work, *Defining Our Own Future: Human Service Leaders on Social Innovation,* leaders in the field supported definitions of social innovation around developing new solutions, but they added their own language related to social enterprise and business, technology integration, and collaboration (Berzin, Pitt-Catsouphes, & Gaitan 2015). Their ideas echoed past definitions but brought to light the challenges of innovating from within the human service sector. Organizational and institutional barriers created difficulties for innovation capacity-building. Resource issues created both an innovation imperative and a set of challenges related to the time, space, and money needed to accomplish the task. But the leaders in the study also showed the potential for innovation to occur within existing organizations given the right resources, time, space, and freedom. Organizations need the right environment but also the right supports to do this effectively. A new understanding of social innovation is needed that incorporates *innovation from within* as a critical pathway and focuses not only on outcomes, but also on the process and tools needed to achieve those outcomes.

Some of the new approaches to social change involve market principles, entrepreneurial thinking, and new venture structures. Entrepreneurship and intrapreneurship provide strategies for transformative change for both new and existing organizations. Social enterprise models use business principles to solve social problems. New organizational models, including social enterprise, social venture, benefit corporations, and social business, redefine the profit and social mission relationship. Existing nonprofits are now leveraging new or hybrid structures to further their mission. Social finance and social impact bonds create new investment opportunities that work to promote social aims. Working as a whole, these innovative mechanisms create a new social sector from which to address social problems. It creates a sector that recognizes multiple pathways to solving social problems and has less concern over revenue structure as a primary determinant of action.

Speaking the Same Language

- *Innovation*: A process, method, product, or outcome that is new and creates an improvement.
- *Social innovation:* An umbrella term that encompasses multiple pathways and processes that address the root causes of social injustices. The solutions are more effective, efficient, and/or sustainable—socially, economically, and environmentally—than previous solutions and are a result of collaboration with diverse stakeholders.
- *Social entrepreneurship*: At its heart is formed by an entrepreneur (typically an individual or small group) starting a business or organization for social purposes. While social entrepreneurship has taken on a broader definition about transformative solutions to social problems using entrepreneurial principles (including risk-taking, innovative approaches, change orientation, and the sustainable business model), it most typically is portrayed as starting or forming something new.
- *Social intrapreneurship*: The use of entrepreneurial principles *within an existing organization or institution* to solve social problems.
- *Social enterprise*: The use of business models or practices to solve social problems. May refer to the socially driven organization or venture that uses market-oriented approaches to achieve its social mission.
- *Social venture*: Refers to an organization (nonprofit, for-profit, or hybrid) that works to achieve a social mission rather than financial gains.
- *Social business*: Refers to an organization that is profit-oriented but has a clear social mission.
- *Benefit corporation (B-corps)*: A type of for-profit entity that pursues social and/or environmental impact missions in addition to financial gain. Shareholders are required to consider the impact of decisions on society in addition to their responsibility to maximize profit.
- *Social finance*: An investment strategy and funding source that simultaneously works to achieve financial gain and social benefit.
- *Social impact bond*: A contract between the government, a social organization, and a private investor. The government agrees to pay the organization for services in exchange for improved social outcomes. Payment does not occur until a predetermined socially beneficial outcome is reached. Investors outside of government are brought in to fund these contracts.
- *Social sector*: Broad range of organizations that are primarily dedicated to social mission, responding to social and/or environmental issues. It includes non-profits, charities, nongovernmental organizations, social enterprises, and social ventures.

The social innovation lexicon represents these multiple approaches and acknowledges the potential for changing the social sector. Equally important is maintaining a steadfast focus on sustainable social change and a propensity toward innovations that enhance social justice. It is this inclusive understanding of social innovation that allows us to look for examples that are not limited solely to the development of new organizations that respond to social problems.

FRAMEWORKS FOR INNOVATION: PARADIGMS, ACTION, AND PROCESS

When we read about social innovation, we are most often met with a range of examples and case studies that show innovation that has already occurred. Research on conceptualizing social innovation focuses on the common features of mission-based outcomes (Dacin, Dacin, & Tracey 2011). Innovation therefore is most readily recognized when an action, such as the development of a new organization, service, program, or product, has occurred. We, however, propose a broader understanding of social innovation outcomes that focuses not only on these action results, but also on shifting paradigms and structures that create transformative social change. This lens implores us to consider social justice in the outcome criteria, and it also broadens the concept of transformational and new responses to social problems by affirming multiple pathways to reach that aim. Social innovation needs to acknowledge innovation outcomes that stretch beyond the typical measures of the development of new products and/or companies. Social innovation can be thought to encompass three possible conceptual frameworks: paradigms, actions, and structures (see Figure 1.1).

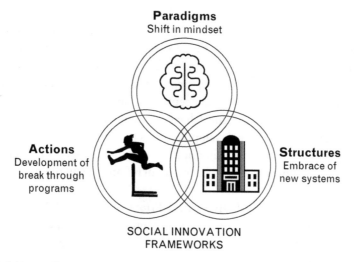

FIGURE 1.1: Social innovation outcomes.

Adapted from Pitt-Catsouphes & Berzin, 2015.

Examples from the Field

Paradigms

Disability Rights Movement shifted our paradigm about equal rights for persons living with disabilities.

Youth Violence as a Public Health Issue transformed our approaches to youth violence and paved the way for prevention and rehabilitation efforts.

Action

Re: Char developed a small system to produce biochar and support farming efficiency.

One Earth Designs developed a solar grill to produce clean energy and respond to fuel scarcity.

Pine Street Inn created a social enterprise program to train homeless individuals and create revenue.

Girls Who Code launched a program to train girls with 21st-century computer skills.

Structure

Rethinking Revenue & Structure allowed service organizations to adopt different structures for supporting clients that challenged traditional service provision and used market practice.

Participant-Directed Care created a new process for people with disabilities to obtain services with greater autonomy and independence.

DISRUPT PARADIGMS FOR BROAD RESULTS

When most people think about innovation, what comes to mind are new programs set up to respond to social issues, groundbreaking products that shift opportunities or provide new solutions, and new organizations that are developed to deliver these programs and products. But some of the most revolutionary innovations have come from shifts in paradigms or thought patterns. Considering *paradigms* as an outcome is about the generation of new ideas, theories, frameworks, or concepts that have the ability to transform the way we understand or examine a social issue. Changes in language or the framing of an issue can be as critical to its solutions as the development of a new program or services. Innovations in thoughts or perspectives radically alter how we consider an issue and therefore open up new possibilities about how we solve it. Examples of reframing paradigms come from across the social service arena.

One example comes from the disability field. Prior to the mid-1900s people with disabilities were considered from the perspective of needing to be treated or fixed. Interventions were designed to separate people with disabilities from society or attempt to cure their limitations. But the disability rights movement drastically shifted that paradigm and paved the way for new policy and practice. The disability rights movement advocated that, although disability is a part of identity, it does not define a person. Someone with a disability can contribute to society and realize their hopes and dreams. To do this requires policy and practice that give people with disabilities equal treatment and equal rights: the right to engage in society, to have equal employment, to have equal educational opportunities, to have equal access to buildings and transportation. This innovation in thought patterns radically shifted how people with disabilities are treated and the services, policies, and accommodations designed to ensure those rights.

A second example relates to the reframing of youth violence as a public health issue. Until the 1980s, youth violence had been viewed as a criminal issue, with responses and solutions that called for incarceration and punishment. Intervention approaches were predicated on crime reduction strategies that said the risk of high levels of punishment would reduce crime. Then, through the pioneering work of Deborah Prothrow-Stith, this issue was reshaped from a criminal issue to a public health problem. She viewed youth violence as a public health issue needing prevention and universal approaches. Recognizing the impact of violence on health and well-being, not only of those involved but also on our communities, called for a complete rethinking of the paradigm and paved the way for different solutions. Solutions to youth crime were now conceived around changing school curriculum, creating developmentally appropriate interventions, broadening participation in prevention efforts, addressing risk factors rather than outcomes, and disseminating information broadly to prevent and intervene on this issue. This innovation in the paradigm of youth violence completely shifted our responses, our interventions, and, ultimately, our solutions. Paradigm shifts are the significant yet underappreciated innovations that open new doors to alternate forms of action.

PRODUCE OUTCOMES THROUGH ACTION

The social innovation dialogue is replete with examples of innovation as action. Action outcomes refer to our common understanding of the launch of new programs, products, or services that respond to a social problem. The social innovation literature is full of examples of individuals creating programs, products, and services that create more effective or more efficient solutions. Efforts like the social enterprises re:Char (http://www.re-char.com/), which sells a small system capable of producing biochar to help farmers grow crops more effectively; and One Earth Designs (https://www.oneearthdesigns.com/), which created a solar grill to support cleaner energy and counter fuel scarcity in the Himalayas, represent product-based innovations. Pine Street Inn (http://www.pinestreetinn.org/), an existing nonprofit homeless organization that created a social enterprise to train individuals transitioning out of homelessness and create revenue and Black Girls Code (http://www.blackgirlscode.com/), a program formed to teach girls of color computer skills that would support employability and diversify the tech field, demonstrate program-based action innovation. These examples and many others represent the possibility of innovation through direct action, services, products, and programs.

As with paradigm shift innovations, structural innovations are less recognized but are consequential in their reach and ability to generate social impact. In the area of *structure,* this approach acknowledges that alternative processes, practices, and organizational structures can meet social need in a transformative way. In this macro paradigm, a shift in structure or process can be equally effective at creating change. Structural or process shifts may occur within existing organizations or programs and may not require the development of new products or services; these approaches instead rely on rethinking how we respond to social needs and shifting those processes.

A significant shift in process innovation comes from new thinking in revenue diversification for nonprofits. New structures allow broader approaches to funding services and create processes that respond to social problems without the need to raise funds through traditional fundraising. *Social enterprise,* defined as applying business models or market-based principles to solving social problems, opened the way for multiple structures and changed the role of service agencies. One such structure, *cross-compensation,* allows for one group of customers to pay for services in part to subsidize these services for another group. A second structure that relates to social enterprise is a process in which employment and skills training is simultaneously used to provide living wages, skills, and job training to the population being served and perhaps revenue to the agency. In a third structure, social enterprises function as the market intermediary (distributing goods for suppliers who are the beneficiaries) or the market connector (facilitating trade relationships between beneficiaries and new markets). In these structures, the beneficiaries—often poor, marginalized, or underrepresented groups—find ways to bring goods to market with the organization playing a market role rather than a traditional service role. These examples are shifting the structure or process by which we respond to social problems and rethink revenue generation.

A second example relates more directly to the provision of services. In traditional service provision for individuals with disabilities, the government or other service provider determines eligibility for and provision of appropriate services. A newer approach, a participant-directed or consumer-directed model (http://www.bc.edu/schools/gssw/nrcpds/), provides services based on the individual's specific needs and requests. This new model of service delivery puts the individual in control. It allows the person in need, rather than social workers or medical professionals, to control all aspects of service provision, including hiring, employee management, deciding on necessary tasks, training, and supervising care workers. This model gives those with disabilities tremendous independence and autonomy in decision-making and specifically lets them direct the type, amount, and source of personal assistance services. While the services received may mimic what would have been ordered by the service agency, the process by which services are chosen and administered is different. It is this process innovation that has brought about significant social impact in this field.

Outcomes across these three domains can meet the criteria for social innovation. In this conceptualization, social innovation is about creating new responses to social problems regardless of approach. Social innovation is about responses that have the potential to transform the problem, the possibility of being sustainable, and the promise of enhancing social justice. Opening our perspective to various approaches to innovation creates enhanced opportunities for solving social problems.

SOLUTIONS FOR INNOVATION: NEW APPROACHES FOR SOLVING PROBLEMS

As social innovation can be thought of using three broad frameworks—shifting paradigms, creating action, and changing structures—it can also be imagined as a range of solutions that are now available to respond to social need. This range of solutions may cause change in paradigm, action, or structure or in multiple approaches at once. Never before in history have we had the potential for so many options to respond. Considered broadly, the exponential growth in knowledge, the ease of global communication, the promise of technology, and the advances in science create the possibility for radical solutions. Yet many remain stuck in definitions of social innovation that only consider creating new programs, products, or organizations.

In a newer approach to social innovation, we must think about a comprehensive range of solutions that exploits what is available. Solutions can be considered that include:

- *Social enterprise*: An income generating or market-based solution can help the sustainability of a program and can even become a job creator for vulnerable populations.
- *Process innovation*: A fresh approach to the way things are done can have a profound influence on your efficiency and effectiveness.
- *Social program:* The nonprofit world is very familiar with developing social programs to empower communities—this is still a tried-and-true avenue for innovation.
- *Benefit corporation (B corps)*: A type of for-profit structure that elevates the company's social mission to the same level of importance as profit. This represents a game-changing framework for businesses.
- *Gamified solution*: Social impact meets fun through gamification. Board games, video games, mobile app games, all are fair game for intervening through entertainment.
- *Media campaign*: A well-designed campaign can generate much-needed awareness and action.
- *Product*: Often overlooked in nonprofit spaces, products can be very effective and practical innovations.
- *Ecological sustainable solution*: An environmental justice lens can help modify what nonprofits are currently doing or will be doing to mitigate our ecological footprint.
- *Nonprofit-for-profit partnership:* Companies who are looking to embrace corporate social responsibility can provide, among other things, resources, guidance, or expertise.
- *Art-based intervention*: Public art, infographics, therapeutic art, music, acting, dance, photography—artistic expression can be a powerful tool for generating social change.
- *Cooperative*: The democratic and collaborative values embedded within co-ops provide a distinctive framework that's invaluable for empowering worker-owners.
- *Traditional nonprofit:* 501c3 status is just one of the benefits of establishing innovations as nonprofits.
- *Policy*: Whether it's an institutional or a government policy, policies have significant influence on the way people think and act.

- *Mobile app*: With smartphones being increasingly ubiquitous, mobile apps can provide a wealth of information in a cost-effective and accessible manner.
- *Educational program:* The way we can open people's minds and expose them to our mission is as diverse as the issues we tackle.
- *Tech-based solutions*: With ongoing technological advances there are infinite ways in which we can integrate technology into nonprofit spaces.
- *Interorganizational collaboration*: A significant strength of the nonprofit sector is our shared vision of social impact. Leverage this goal to collaborate and scale our impact.

PATHWAYS TO INNOVATION: ENTREPRENEURSHIP AND INTRAPRENEURSHIP

As we consider different social innovation outcomes, it is equally important to consider the path or process by which we achieve innovation. While innovation through entrepreneurship is critical, it would be short-sighted to underestimate the talent, resources, and potential contributions that existing organizations have to offer social innovation. Existing nonprofit organizations bring with them deep-rooted expertise and knowledge about populations and social problems, social capital and relationships, resources, and organizational infrastructure. Utilizing these assets will amplify opportunities to develop, scale, and sustain social innovation. It is therefore critical to understand that there are multiple pathways to innovation and to recognize the challenges and strengths associated with each.

The majority of literature, media attention, and acknowledgment of innovation comes from the lens of social entrepreneurship. This approach has produced such world-altering innovations as Grameen Bank's solution of microfinance, Room to Read's innovation that brings literacy to underprivileged children, and Barefoot College's novel approach to bringing self-sufficiency and sustainability to impoverished rural communities.

Social entrepreneurship at its heart is formed by an entrepreneur (typically an individual or small group) starting a business or organization for social purpose. While social entrepreneurship has taken on a broader definition about transformative solutions to social problems using entrepreneurial principles (including risk-taking, innovative approaches, change orientation, sustainable business model), it most typically is portrayed as starting or forming something new.

These efforts are laudable, and social entrepreneurship has been recognized through multiple organizations dedicated to supporting, sustaining, and celebrating individual achievement for social good. The list of organizations and opportunities celebrating and supporting social entrepreneurs continues to grow. Each organization finds extraordinary people doing extraordinary things. This work remains an important part of social problem-solving.

Examples from the Field

Organizations Recognizing Social Entrepreneurs

Ashoka, one of the world's first social entrepreneurship organizations, has recognized close to 3,000 social entrepreneurship fellows, creating a vast network of knowledge sharing and exchange (https://www.ashoka.org).

Schwab Foundation for Social Entrepreneurship has a global network of social entrepreneurs working to advance innovative models and be a catalyst for change (http://www.schwabfound.org/).

Encore.org focuses on older social entrepreneurs, building a movement that leverages the talent and experience of people in midlife and beyond (http://encore.org/).

Skoll Foundation has invested more than $400 million and recognized 108 entrepreneurs with a goal of increasing impact through examining issue ecosystems and maximizing impact (http://www.skollfoundation.org/).

Poptech focuses on interdisciplinary collaboration, bringing together innovators from across disciplines to cultivate exchange and curate ideas for lasting impact (http://poptech.org/).

Echoing Green has invested more than $36 million in 600 early-stage social entrepreneurs to support seed funding for their initiatives (http://www.echoinggreen.org/).

But this approach is not without challenges. Entrepreneurship is not for everyone, and it is not always the answer. For many social ventures, failure is inevitable, with real cost and impact for the field. The elevated risk in entrepreneurship has added meaning in the social sector, when our successes and failures have a direct impact on the communities we serve. While sustainability and scale are insurmountable barriers for a majority of new entrepreneurial endeavors, existing nonprofit organizations demonstrate significant potential in that, thanks to their longevity, these are issues that have already been overcome.

Given the challenges of entrepreneurship and the potential capacities that can be leveraged from existing agencies, an alternative path to innovation is promising. Intrapreneurship has been more narrowly defined as working on behalf of an existing organization that takes on the responsibility and risk for developing an idea so that it can become a new product or service (Pinchot & Pellman 1999). In a broader sense, intrapreneurship refers to the use of an entrepreneurial approach within an existing organizational structure. Promoting intrapreneurship means building and nourishing innovation capacity within existing organizations—and it also means leveraging what's already there. There are compelling reasons to support social intrapreneurship as a complementary path to innovation.

Social intrapreneurship is the use of entrepreneurial principles within an existing organization or institution to solve social problems. It speaks to the integration of innovation, risk-taking, and initiative to seek new solutions, products, or services *within* an existing organization. It can refer to an individual or small group, but also to the intrapreneurial mindset in which existing organizations continue to innovate. Intrapreneurship is about developing, implementing, and sustaining innovation *within existing* organizations.

RECOGNIZE THAT WE ARE NOT
ALL ENTREPRENEURS

This country has growing interest in entrepreneurship, with more than 13% of Americans reporting early-stage entrepreneurial activity (starting a venture or running a business less than 3.5 years old; Singer, Amorós, & Moska 2015). Although this is a high figure, that still leaves another 87% of people with a different mindset. How could it be that the only people who can solve social problems successfully are in the 13%?

In its broadest definition, "entrepreneurship is the process by which individuals pursue opportunities without regard to the resources they currently control" (Stevenson 1983). This definition suggests that there are entrepreneurs everywhere, wanting to pursue opportunities but perhaps not engaged in starting brand-new ventures. How much different would our solutions look if we could harness the power of all people toward social problem-solving? Recognizing that there are multiple paths to innovation suggests that solutions need to come from outside early-stage entrepreneurial activities, but include all people who want to solve social problems.

SPEND TIME DOING, NOT BUILDING

A significant challenge of entrepreneurship is the focus on organizational development. Each of the organizations that is celebrated in the media with accolades or awards represents a successful startup. But what we don't often think or hear about is the difficulty in starting and sustaining these organizations. We do not think about all of the ideas and startup ventures that do not make it to fruition. New social ventures (whether for-profit, nonprofit, or hybrids) are likely to fail at the same rate as other new for-profit organizations (an estimated 34% survive after 10 years; Bureau of Labor Statistics 2016). Social entrepreneurs are solving problems related to populations who need support the most. Ill-fated attempts that either do not work or cannot be sustained may lead to more problems and discouragement for the communities that were the target of intervention.

Conversely, existing organizations have structures that have withstood the test of time and are in a position to initiate something new because they have already proved they can. They have weathered the storm of difficult financial times and adjusted to changes in demand or need. They understand the social problem and the market where that problem exists. The best nonprofits know how to successfully anticipate cash flow, navigate growth, and position their product. Management effectiveness and operational efficiency have carried them to maturity, positioning them to engage in new efforts in a way that new companies cannot.

Existing organizations are able to spend time doing the work because they have already made it through the building phase. There is no need to reinvent, recreate, or build infrastructure. Instead, time and resources can be spent on projects that solve problems rather than building infrastructure. Many argue that there are enough nonprofits; quality is needed, not quantity. Supporting existing organizations toward innovation means less energy in the sector is spent on building and more time is spent on responding to challenges.

STARTING AND SUSTAINING ARE NOT THE SAME

While it may seem obvious that skill sets vary by profession, we often underestimate the distinct characteristics needed to accomplish tasks within one profession. Even for those ventures that are successful, a distinct skill set is related to startup that is not the same skill set needed for maintenance or sustaining. Some individuals are serial entrepreneurs who love to look at problems and build solutions. They do not want to focus and set down roots in one area or one venture. For these social entrepreneurs, their skills related to solution generation, business modeling, and launching are critical for new organizations. But the activities of long-term success and sustainability require a different skill set or perhaps even a different leader. The nimble flexibility of a new venture may not be effective as organizations scale and attempt to spread their innovation. We are used to rewarding startups, but not recognizing or acknowledging the skill sets and know-how necessary to sustain a nonprofit. A founder's attributes may not be the right characteristics for ensuring the longevity of an innovation. Intrapreneurship leverages not only the founder mentality of people within an organization who can develop an idea, but also the management skill sets needed to grow and sustain it.

EXPAND IMPACT BY GOING TO SCALE

When ventures are successful, a next step is often to consider how to scale. For many entrepreneurial endeavors, this is a problem because founders are unable to replicate their program or successfully integrate it into another community. People talk about the inability to "replicate" the founder: because of heavy reliance on the entrepreneur, the venture could not possibly be launched in another community without another such individual. This is not to say that there are not many social entrepreneurs who take their organization, product, or idea to scale. But, for others, this is a significant hurdle. Dees and Anderson talk about broadening definitions of scaling by considering alternative approaches to spreading impact, like dissemination, affiliation, and branching (Dees & Anderson 2004). They suggest defining the innovation in a way that supports not only scaling the organization, but also scaling the idea.

Scaling Impact

Dissemination: Sharing ideas, tools, and resources to scale
Affiliation: Creating a network of affiliated programs that have to adhere to particular standards, principles, or practices to use the brand
Branching: Developing local branches of a central organization

---

For existing organizations that have been around and already worked with whole communities nationally or even globally, scaling is part of what they do.
They have infrastructure and may already work across the spectrum of a specific problem or across multiple populations facing related issues. A startup has to worry about how to

grow, how to scale, and how to translate its successes to new populations or new locations. Existing organizations may not face this challenge in the same way. Within nonprofits, it is not about how to grow the innovation or how to reach a larger set of people, but, in fact, it's how to innovate that it is the challenge. Capitalizing on their successful scale may mean bringing innovation to a larger set of people more quickly.

LEVERAGE EXISTING EXPERTISE

It may sound simple, but smart people work at existing agencies. It would be short-sighted to believe that all of the good ideas come from people who work outside the field. *Open innovation* touts the idea of recognizing intelligence and capacity from the outside, but we also need to recognize what exists within our organizations. People trained to work in nonprofits and social services bring significant expertise and training to their work. It would be a tremendous oversight to not attempt to harness and support existing nonprofit leaders in developing and implementing innovation. These individuals have worked with the problems that social innovation hopes to overcome and the populations that social innovation seeks to support, and they have a unique take on their organization's actions and relationships. Their knowledge and experience should prove invaluable to the social innovation paradigm and to ultimately developing the most powerful solutions.

> *Open innovation* is the power to harness external ideas and approaches to further the mission of the organization by engaging the public as well as other organizations in idea generation.

Existing agencies may not be organized to leverage this creativity. Their staff is often so consumed with getting the work done, overcoming challenges, responding to crisis, and stretching resources that innovation feels like a luxury. Innovation has a tendency to feel beyond their scope or charge. But what if we could train people and retool agencies? What if we could create a movement that supported existing agencies to become innovative? What if we could create organizations that could innovate not once, but over and over again? These agencies could harness all of the potential that exists within the staff and leadership of their organizations.

DISTRIBUTE LEADERSHIP FOR SUSTAINABILITY

Another resource of existing agencies is their diverse leadership. Existing nonprofits already have multiple leaders, teams, and staff. This brings a variety of viewpoints, but also multiple individuals to enhance innovation and creativity. Diverse teams often yield the most creative outcomes. While entrepreneurship is often contingent on one charismatic leader to ensure the success of the venture, continued success may be reliant on the person's involvement or on being able to find someone as good and as passionate. There are benefits of leadership diffusion that allow multiple stakeholders to be connected and committed to the effort. *Innovation from within* can be initiated by leadership at various levels within the organization. Thanks to leadership diffusion that naturally exists within most nonprofits, multiple people are able to champion and sustain new innovation efforts. Figuring out how to utilize this resource becomes the challenge for moving from the status quo to innovation.

UTILIZE THE POWER
OF ORGANIZATIONAL ASSETS

Existing organizations also bring infrastructure and social capital to the endeavor. Their developed administration, marketing, and staff resources mean less duplication and time spent building these assets. Relationships and social assets may lead to collaborative innovations and/or partnerships with the private and public sectors. Even name recognition and the branding of existing organizations should be considered a resource to exploit for developing, implementing, and sustaining innovation. The existing donor base and government contracts may support the organization and help catalyze innovation. Board members bring expertise, relationships, and resources. All of these established networks and assets should be leveraged for innovation.

CREATE SUSTAINABILITY FOR IMPACT

A lot of attention in the entrepreneurship literature focuses on how new organizations build for sustainability. But what really counts in the social sector is not just starting, but *sustaining*. It is not just about having an idea, but about bringing it to scale and sustaining it over time. Existing nonprofits bring a proven track record of sustainability. Their history of sustainability and their ability to survive across different social, economic, and political times supports their ability to bring innovation not just through the development and implementation stages, but over the long haul. Having survived financial downturns and economic instability, having responded at times of pressure and crisis, having the right leadership, and having demonstrated success during challenges, existing nonprofits have proved they can sustain. It may require diversifying revenue streams or programming or regrouping in times of austerity, but these organizations have been around for many years. This proven record of sustainability means they can continue to thrive, not just start innovations but sustain them.

These attributes position existing agencies as strong contributors to a new social innovation paradigm that benefits from their organizational and human capital assets. Intrapreneurship becomes an important and viable path to social innovation. Social innovation today must be defined to include process and outcomes that take advantage of multiple approaches to innovation. Only then can we leverage all resources toward solving social problems.

REFLECTION FOR REFRAMING SOCIAL INNOVATION

1. Consider examples from your own work or organization that encompass different social innovation outcomes.
2. Consider innovations that relate to the social issue you care most about. Can you name examples that represent changes in paradigm, structure, and action?
3. Think about one of the solution options presented in the chapter that is least often utilized in your field (e.g., gamified solution, B-corp, art-based intervention) and consider how it could be used.
4. Reflect on an intrapreneurial effort you have been engaged in or read or heard about. What were the benefits over starting a new organization? What were the challenges? Did the effort leverage any of the elements discussed in this chapter?

MAIN POINTS FOR REFRAMING SOCIAL INNOVATION

- Social innovation is a field-changing paradigm that brings new tools to the process of problem-solving, brings new players to addressing social need, and opens the range of solutions that may be considered.
- The definition of "social innovation" encompasses both outcome and process. While definitions of the term vary, social innovation creates new, effective, sustainable, just solutions through creativity and collaboration to advance a social issue.
- Rather than just the development of a new product or program, social innovation is also the process itself. Social innovation can come in the form of shifting paradigms, structures, or action.
- Solutions may encompass traditional and nontraditional approaches to solving social injustice, including integration of new technology, arts-based initiatives, development of social enterprises, programmatic improvements, or media campaigns.
- Entrepreneurship and intrapreneurship are complementary paths to innovation—both should be pursued and recognized. Intrapreneurship provides the lens for existing organizations to pursue social innovation and leverage existing resources.

CLAIM THE NONPROFIT ROLE IN INNOVATION

Chapter 2 asserts the demand for nonprofit engagement in innovation, but also recognizes the unique contributions that nonprofits make to this work.

Get ready to ...

1. Recognize the urgency for innovation in today's nonprofits.
2. Leverage your assets as a nonprofit to engage in innovation work.
3. Discover the *Nonprofit Innovation Model.*

In redefining social innovation, it is clear that existing agencies have a role to play and a contribution to make. But in the nonprofit context, there are unique opportunities and challenges that have led some to question the relevance of social innovation, others to view themselves outside the social innovation field, and others to engage wholeheartedly in an attempt to stay ahead of the curve. These questions about social innovation's relevance to existing nonprofits and their potential engagement fuel a discussion about the very role and future of the sector. Understanding social innovation's definition and broadening its application have important consequences for individual organizations and the sector as a whole. But to engage in a meaningful way also requires an acknowledgment of the specific context of innovation within existing nonprofits and specific processes that support their full inclusion.

Our work with nonprofit and for-profit partners has affirmed the need for innovation. It has shown us a set of common challenges that stand in the way of nonprofit innovation, but it has also enlightened us about unsung facilitators. Capitalizing on these often hidden assets allows organizations to do more with what they have. Developing and testing our innovation processes has given us insight into what works with agencies on the ground. And all of these experiences have confirmed the potential for existing agencies to successfully engage in innovation processes and develop radical solutions.

While building innovation capacity is critical, it is important to acknowledge the tremendous capacity for innovation that nonprofits have shown throughout history. Nonprofits have served our most vulnerable populations and have continued to reinvent new solutions in the face of extreme challenges, varied social conditions, and changing economic times. Many of the social challenges we have solved or social conditions that have been improved came from the work of the sector. Policy and practice that have worked to eradicate child labor in the United States, guaranteed free and equal education, identified and developed a child protective system, create supports for the elderly and for people with physical, developmental, and mental health disabilities have come from innovations within the sector. While we recognize that important history, this section pushes us to reconsider how to build on existing capacity and amplify impact through enhanced readiness for innovation. This chapter challenges nonprofits to think about the imperative of innovation and explores the reality of both the opportunities and challenges it presents. The chapter concludes by outlining the Nonprofit Innovation Model (IN Model), a model developed specifically for innovation within nonprofits that exploits the resources of existing organizations.

CALL TO ACTION: WHY NONPROFITS MUST INNOVATE

Leaders of today's nonprofit and human service organizations face some challenging realities. They are faced with increasingly complex social problems, declining resources, and expanding competition. The blurred boundaries between for-profit and nonprofit entities create challenges and opportunities as collaborations create shared resources and talent, but also competition for attention. Globalization and technology provide challenges, but also opportunities to support an innovation environment. Opportunities exist for knowledge growth and development, retraining, and learning from outside the sector. Nonprofits must embrace an innovation mentality to respond to these challenges and take advantage of these opportunities. This section explores the necessity of innovation given this context.

CHALLENGE OURSELVES TO DO BETTER

Perhaps there is no more compelling reason to engage in innovation than the social problems we continue to face. Let's face it—we work with complex, challenging problems. There are problems that have existed for hundreds of years and problems that continue to emerge. There are issues related to poverty, violence, and health and wellness that are intertwined and multidimensional and for which full solutions have yet to be articulated. These *wicked problems* have elusive solutions with complex interconnections, large economic costs, and huge population impact. There are also emergent problems that relate to our changing demography and shifting environmental context. These problems are new, and we have not yet grappled with their solutions.

In the State of the Sector Survey, more than 80% of respondents reported an increase in demand for services, and a majority reported being unable to meet these demands (Nonprofit Finance Fund 2014). New strategies and approaches are needed to be able to cope with these demands.

Trends that will shape the next century, including the demographic-social-economic diaspora, new roles of civil society, changes in food supply and demand, threats to the ecosystem, and changes in longevity, health, social interactions, and human development create both new opportunities and challenges for the sector (Johansen 2009). The confluence of these and other trends, such as the continuing increase in economic inequalities, means that many social problems will become even more complex. Some argue that because traditional approaches have not produced desired results, adding new competencies to social sector organizations may result in improved service delivery models (Dart 2004). Human service organizations are driven by their desire to improve outcomes and change the lives of vulnerable populations. There is a need in the field to go beyond low-impact, short-term strategies and instead think about bold, transformative impact. These challenges provide the motivation to do more; to use all available resources, knowledge, and tools to solve social problems.

FACE THE COMPETITION

Innovation also provides a competitive advantage as we consider the competitive context of today's nonprofit sector. The nonprofit sector represents close to 2.3 million nonprofit organizations, including the 1.58 million nonprofits registered with the IRS (Pettijohn 2013). The largest category, 501(c)(3) public charities, represent close to 1 million (Blackwood, Pettijohn, & Roeger 2012). The sector employs nearly 10.7 million paid workers, making it just over 10% of our country's total private employment and the third largest employer among US industries (Salamon, Sokolowski, & Gellar 2012). The nonprofit sector has faced tremendous growth, creating jobs and more economic opportunities than any other sector in a comparable time period (Salamon et al. 2012). While the 60% growth of reporting nonprofits (those with 501(c)(3) status; Wing, Roeger, & Pollack 2010) represents tremendous achievement for the sector, it also creates competition for investment and philanthropic dollars.

Nonprofit growth not only means more solutions, but also more infrastructure and more organizations to support. For the individual and private donor, new organizations also mean more places to diversify giving. It means that the existing contracts and philanthropic dollars get spread among additional staff, buildings, programming, and technology, sometimes funding duplicative services. It means more competition for staff and for human resource supports. Coupled with underinvestment in leadership development, it means nonprofits compete not only for finances, but also for leadership. Competing with additional nonprofits may threaten the long-term viability of some in the face of these limited resources.

This increased competition and this proliferation of nonprofits may help strengthen our ability to solve social problems and respond to demand, but it may also lack long-term sustainability because smaller organizations cannot compete. It suggests a need for nonprofits to build administrative capabilities, to work together through collaboration, and to remain innovative to stay relevant.

DO MORE WITH LESS

You cannot mention nonprofits without a follow-up statement that somehow reflects the decline in resources, the drive for financial sustainability, or the tremendous resources devoted to fundraising. More options for supporting social causes create competition for traditional resource acquisition. Funding needs are a reality that is here to stay. Nonprofit resources are becoming scarcer as the nonprofit sector is expected to do more with less.

The economic recession created significant declines in the funding of health and human services. When economic times are more difficult, services get cut. State funding declined for many social sector agencies, with funding cuts in public health spending for 31 states, in services to elderly and disabled individuals in 29 states, and in education in 34 states (Johnson, Oliff, & Williams 2011). Even with postrecession restoration of some spending, spending rates remain more than 3% below prerecession 2008 spending (Husch 2011). Foundations that provide grants, including family, community, and corporate foundations, also remain below prerecession giving rates (Lawrence & Mukai 2011). The sector simply has higher needs to contend with and fewer resources.

Additionally, the sector faces challenges to traditional giving, with charity spread among a wider set of avenues (see the box "New Options for Supporting Social Causes"). New vehicles for giving may be a win for existing nonprofits or may draw funds away from traditional agencies and toward nimble start-ups or smaller, more individualized causes. Philanthropy plays out across multiple recipients, and existing agencies have to compete to keep their donor base.

New Options for Supporting Social Causes

Cause marketing: Marketing efforts that pair for-profit businesses with nonprofit organizations/causes to raise money for the company and cause and increase awareness

Crowdfunding: Raising money from a large number of individuals, often making use of the Internet or social media

Impact investing: Investing in companies that create environmental or social benefit in addition to financial return

Social venture capital: Using seed funding investments in social enterprises to achieve financial gain and social impact

Venture philanthropy: Typically involves targeting resources (grants or investments) to a particular systemic issue with a longer period of investment and intensive engagement between the investor and recipient

---

Traditional donors (individuals and foundations) are finding other ways to generate social and environmental impact through nontraditional vehicles. Converting donations into investment strategies through impact investing takes money from the sector and may diminish the purely altruistic motivations of philanthropy. Providing seed funding through social venture capital investments favors social sector work that occurs through social enterprise models. Venture philanthropy's emphasis on large, targeted, systemic engagements supports social change but moves funds from traditional nonprofits and service work.

Examples from the Field

Crowdfunding

Parkinson's Institute and Clinical Center is an independent nonprofit agency dedicated to providing patient care and clinical and basic research for Parkinson's disease.

While they provide services and do traditional fundraising, the Institute recently completed the most successfully funded health campaign on crowdfunding site Indiegogo.

They launched their crowdfunding campaign with a $100,000 match from the Draper Foundation, followed by a second $100,000 match from a board member, and, within three months, raised more than $500,000 through crowdfunding site Indiegogo.

Cause Marketing

DoSomething.org is a nonprofit aimed at engaging young people to make changes through campaigns for social impact. They teamed up with Aéropostale department store to encourage young people to drop off used jeans that would be donated to homeless youth. The program brought additional teens to the popular clothing store.

Cause marketing competes with traditional philanthropy in that people perceive that they have donated to charity when only small percentages of their purchase actually go to the cause. Research confirms that people give less to charity subsequent to buying cause marketing products (Krishna 2011). Donors who give through these sources limit traditional giving as they view these gifts as part of an overall charitable giving strategy.

Furthermore, the new breed of donor expects more transparency and greater input on spending. Donors want to know exactly what the money is being spent on and want to be sure their donations are being used to respond to their interests. Crowdfunding websites, which share details about exactly how funds will be used for specific projects, let donors at all levels feel connected to the causes they are supporting. As a $5.1 billion industry (Massolution 2013), crowdfunding raises far less money than nonprofits in the United States (approximately $300 billion; Giving USA 2016), yet nonprofit giving is not growing and crowdfunding is. Crowdfunding projects may figure less in terms of administrative cost and overhead, and, while relatively small compared to nonprofits, they are competing for the same donors.

Competition for scarce resources places a burden on existing organizations. Innovative organizations may be better able to compete with newer, more nimble entities. Innovation can also help organizations learn to seamlessly navigate public-private-nonprofit partnerships, adjust their organizational structures to respond to funding needs, and be open to more creative funding approaches that lead to greater long-term success.

CAPITALIZE ON ERODING BOUNDARIES

In part, as revenue sources shift for nonprofits, the traditional categories for nonprofit entities are also shifting. This also provides motivation to innovate. Nonprofits are no longer able to operate under traditional boundaries and as closed entities. Relying exclusively on grants or government contracts no longer works as these income sources decrease and are shared by more players. These traditional contract-based models limit the ability of organizations to be financially sustainable. Furthermore, these funding streams allow for little time, space, or resources devoted to innovation because they are often based on payment for services rendered. Instead, the next generation of the field necessitates collaboration, new financial structures, and adapted models.

In this complex environment, solving social problems requires all hands on deck—government, business, and nonprofits. It requires new cross-sector partnerships and leaders who can fluidly work across boundaries. It is impossible to imagine solving today's toughest social, environmental, and health challenges by working in isolation. *Collective impact* is the commitment of a group of people from different sectors coming together under a common agenda to solve a particular social problem. To create, coordinate, and scale social impact requires this cross-sector collaboration. On an organizational level, strategic alliances and cross-sector collaboration also serve the individual nonprofit. Collaboration across and within the sector has significant implications for financial sustainability, service delivery, shared expertise, and social impact.

Removing strict sectoral boundaries not only paves the way for collaboration, but it also helps us rethink the very meaning of "nonprofit." Nonprofits are defined by the fact that revenue is not dispersed to owners but instead is reinvested into the mission, and this fact carries with it particular tax implications. In the broader lexicon, "nonprofit" has taken on the meaning of being associated with charitable organizations and therefore social good. As we begin to break down sectoral boundaries, organizations that work for social good no longer need to be considered solely in the nonprofit space. We open the door for considering hybrid or for-profit structures that also achieve social mission. Social enterprise models, which marry business principles and market-based approaches to solving social problems, are increasingly utilized in the sector. Social enterprises are businesses that use commercial strategies to achieve social mission but can be structured as for-profit or nonprofit. Commonly, social enterprises either employ hard-to-employ populations or use an earned revenue strategy to support their mission. Government policy that allows the use of benefit corporations and low-profit limited liability corporations (L3C) supports this aim (Berzin, Pitt-Catsouphes, & Peterson 2014). Nonprofit organizations need to understand these innovative approaches to compete for resources, but also to leverage all possible approaches to support their mission.

Other trends also support blurred sectoral boundaries and the need for innovation. The increased privatization of public services and government contracting add

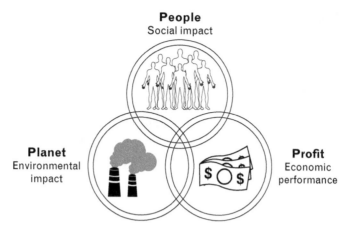

People
Social impact

Planet
Environmental
impact

Profit
Economic
performance

FIGURE 2.1: Triple bottom line.

to the momentum of social entrepreneurship and management innovation (Chell, Nicolopoulou, & Karatas-Ozkan 2010).

Corporate social responsibility, aimed at assessing and regulating corporate impact on social and environmental outcomes, suggests a new breed of company with greater attention paid to social impact. These examples and others, including microfinance, sustainable business, social investing, and other avenues that promote a triple bottom line related to profit, people, and planet, suggest an emergent new sector that integrates social impact with business (Sabeti & Fourth Sector Network Concept Working Group 2009) (see Figure 2.1). This fourth sector requires new thinking for the nonprofit sector and provides new opportunities for innovation.

GO GLOBAL

Ongoing and increasing globalization is a megatrend that influences not only the economic structures of the future, but also trends in communication, global problem-solving, and sustainability. Nonprofit organizations need to be ready to respond to the added complexities and opportunities that this presents, and innovation can support this aim. The networking opportunities now made available through social media, multinational organizations, and broad membership organizations are immense. We are now able to build broader coalitions than ever before to amplify our voice and share key resources. Examples of this range from the adaptation of microfinance models around the world and the viral impact of the Ice Bucket Challenge to the remarkable spread of action during social movements like the Arab Spring and the Black Lives Matter movement born in Ferguson, Missouri.

Of equal relevance is the ability of nonprofits to maximize on a larger donor base. Globalization has opened new markets for microentreprenuers in developing countries to connect with new customers. It has allowed donors to be able to engage with international nonprofits on a different level. The public is also developing a growing interest in and awareness of the ethical sourcing of products being consumed. The pressure for accountability that consumers can have on corporations has tremendous potential. Thanks to this force, trends such as fair and direct trade practice, sweatshop-free products, and the Kimberley Process for diamonds have become more central to international business practices. Nonprofits are at the root of community development and sustainability practices. We must be a part of this conversation and action.

In addition to creating multiple opportunities for growth, trends in globalization have created a new context that nonprofits around the world must respond to. Increased rates of immigration have changed the population demographics of many nonprofits. This presents new cultural considerations including different language, gender, traditional, and religious customs. Nonprofits must be able to identify and adapt to this new cultural context in order to remain effective and inclusive.

EXPLOIT THE POWER OF TECHNOLOGY

The link between innovation and technology is palpable. Information and communications technology (ICT) provides promise, opportunity, and possibility. It is changing the world and changing the way people do business. It opens opportunities for spreading programs and services, for greater impact, and for global communication and connection. Information technology creates tremendous opportunities for management and administrative practices, research, and the use of big data. Social media creates new social opportunities and changes the relationships people have with each other. There is an intimate link between technology and innovation, and nonprofit organizations have an opportunity and responsibility to harness this connection.

The sheer number of people using technology translates into millions of potential consumers of social services and unending opportunities for engagement. According to GSMA, by the end of 2013, 3.4 billion unique subscribers were using mobile technology (GSMA 2014). This represents 47% of people on the planet, many of whom previously had few ways to connect. The web provides instantaneous and global connection. Advances in adaptive technologies, accessibility, and assistive features provide access to people across a range of disabilities. The access to diverse populations offers the promise of new solutions to social problems. Nonprofit organizations can leverage technology to reach new communities, obtain concrete data, and develop innovative solutions.

Examples from the Field

Technology

Big data: The City of Buffalo uses city-level data to inform neighborhood outreach and target employment services.

Social media: Forefront: Innovations in Suicide Prevention launched Facebook collaboration for suicide prevention and support.

Mobile technology: Monterey Bay Aquarium developed a mobile app, Seafood Watch, to support sustainable seafood purchases.

Robotics: RP-7i Remote Presence medical robot connects patients who need specialized care with long-distance physicians.

Gamification: Urban Ministries of Durham developed the game "Spent" to provide awareness about the lives of homeless individuals.

Web 2.0 tools: One state child welfare agency uses technology-related tools, including a research blog, vlogs, and cloud-based documents to enhance model fidelity to a family group decision-making intervention.

Texting: The Crisis Text Line has a staff of trained counselors who offer free and anonymous support 24/7 for teens who are experiencing suicidal ideation.

Management applications: Community TechKnowledge supports more than 18,000 nonprofits with management tools around client outcomes, grants, and victim support.

There is an opportunity to create a paradigm shift in the sector, one that views technology as imperative, not an extraneous tool or one that is too difficult or too costly to implement. New technology has become accessible, easy to use, and often inexpensive. The sheer number of uses for technology in the sector is astounding.

Big data can become the pathway to understanding complex problems in new ways. Real-time assessment and intervention can take place using mobile technology. Social media can be harnessed to connect isolated communities and intervene across large social networks. Robotics can simulate particular roles or be used for teaching. Gamification opens new entry points for reaching younger consumers, motivating behavior, or for practicing skill sets. For management, technology provides the promise of cost-savings and efficiency, including the use of Web 2.0 tools (Sage 2014). These represent just a fraction of technology applications that could respond to social problems. An innovation approach opens the field to more actively engage with information and communication technology to develop new solutions.

LEARN FROM PRIVATE INDUSTRY

While perhaps not a motivator for innovation, the work of the for-profit sector may provide important lessons. Nonprofits may need convincing about how to integrate innovation strategies into their already full agenda, but the for-profit industry has always invested in the power of innovation. Savvy businesses recognize that innovation is not only a possibility, but an imperative. The most innovative companies seamlessly reinvent themselves and launch new products from within their walls. They capitalize on open innovation strategies to utilize external talent and assets; they support internal innovation through innovation departments, competitions, and positions; and they build innovation into the company's DNA through policy mechanisms and employee compensation. Private industry recognizes that good ideas can and should be harnessed from the inside as well. And when they do, they use this to make their company stronger and more successful, not necessarily to start new companies. When Apple went from a computer company to a music store to a phone producer, no one said it had to take place by forming new companies. When Google went from a search engine to a mapping company to an operating system to a data source, no one said it could only be done through new companies. When Bill Gates wants innovation at Microsoft, he reviews staff business plans for launching new ideas. We need to bring this *innovation from within* mindset to the nonprofit sector. We need to capitalize on existing organizational assets and strengths to bring bold, new ideas to fruition and to help them endure.

Nonprofits are interested in practice improvements and shrinking the impact of social problems; innovation serves as a mechanism to get there. The areas outlined in this section serve as important stimulus to moving time and resources toward innovation.

OPPORTUNITIES AND CHALLENGES: INNOVATION IN THE NONPROFIT CONTEXT

While nonprofits may be motivated toward innovation, the unique nonprofit context creates opportunities and challenges. In today's environment, innovation is everywhere. It is an imperative for private industry and a buzzword for government. Innovation is a label for how you work and for the outcomes you seek to achieve. We are all motivated by the battle cry to "be more innovative," "think out of the box," and "harness our creative energy," yet we rarely are given tools to accomplish this or strategies for overcoming the obstacles to innovation that exist in the nonprofit world.

A lot of innovation work assumes that innovation takes place outside the organizational context (often with a startup mentality) and through individual champions pioneering change without organizational obstacles. Examples of successful innovations often share their outcomes without a lens into process. Still other innovation stories are embedded in a for-profit context, with its distinct challenges and opportunities. But the nonprofit sector brings with it a unique context for innovation. It is a sector with more than 10 million people working in close to 1.5 million organizations (Roeger, Blackwood, & Pettijohn 2012), and these organizations share some commonalities. This is not to say that all nonprofit experiences are the same and that there are no similarities across sectors, but nonprofits bring a specific vantage point to innovation work. Discovering the specificities of doing innovation work in this context enhances our ability to act.

Nonprofits that want to engage in innovation recognize some significant challenges of doing this work:

- Limited resources for investment and overhead
- Resistance to change
- Competing priorities

But they also recognize that their organizations bring assets to the table:

- Steadfast commitment to a shared mission
- Diverse board
- Strong community relationships
- Social sector knowledge and expertise
- Established structures, processes, and human capital

Nonprofits that successfully engage in social innovation leverage these strengths and take the time to recognize and work through these challenges.

FIND THE MONEY

The nonprofit context is replete with challenges related to funding. Nonprofits continually have to justify expenses and do more with fewer resources. With current nonprofit paradigms dissuading organizations from investing in themselves, resources being used for anything other than program expenditure are often seen as waste (Pallotta 2008). By comparison, for-profit spending in innovation and R&D has continued to grow, reaching an all-time high of $647 billion among the Global Innovation 1000 companies (Jaruzelski, Schwartz, & Staack 2015).

In the nonprofit context, the path to innovation and research funds is not nearly as apparent. Nonprofits have more difficulty finding funds to invest in overhead, research, or new initiatives; instead, funds are accounted for in program spending and are often for restricted use.

So then, how can we actually go about funding innovation in the nonprofit sector? Considering specific fundraising efforts tied to innovation, engaging specific board members in raising capital for an innovation effort, or expanding to new avenues for revenue might create the seed funding to do innovation work. Social impact bonds and competitive innovation funding might also provide new pots of money to explore innovation.

Even when funds are not readily available, we need to stop thinking of innovation as only occurring when we have dedicated money. Innovation must be part of the culture of how the organization operates. It must be baked into the processes and the environment. Innovation must be a strategic priority. It should happen from the way you bring people together, the way you solicit ideas, the tools you use, and the vision you promote. To truly make a shift toward innovation, nonprofits need to capitalize on all opportunities for innovation and to begin to see innovation work as being as critical to their overhead as other elements.

BEAT THE NAYSAYERS

Engaging in innovation will always be met with some resistance. It is nearly impossible to get everyone on board with something—particularly something new or different. The organizational change literature is clear—organizations are often resistant to change (Agocs 1997; Gilley, Godek, & Gilley 2009; Van de Ven & Sun 2011). And this can be even more true of nonprofit organizations. Nonprofits tend to be risk-averse. There is a tremendous concern over doing something new because the risks are high. Different from a for-profit that is primarily taking a financial risk, nonprofits may feel that they are taking a chance with a person's life. If innovation does not work, the stakes are too high, the consequences could be dire. So, how do we move beyond this? How do we challenge the status quo and take risks?

Communication. Communication. Communication. Innovation is not about doing secret research in a back room and unveiling a new product or service. It is about opening avenues to share and improve on ideas. Finding ways to involve the whole organization in innovation efforts, even if only a few are directly involved. Letting people know it is happening and being open to having hard discussions. Challenging the status quo is difficult, but if you do not engage in innovation, if do not try to improve services and solve problems, the consequences can also be dire. We face continued problems, expanding populations to serve, and limited resources available to fulfill the need. Innovation provides new possibilities for how we can approach these issues. Even the naysayers should be on board with that.

Innovation is about taking small or calculated risks. It is about failing often and early when the stakes are low. As nonprofits begin to build innovation into their DNA, these small failures (and the lessons that come from them) become a part of how work is done. Gaining experience with risk-taking, practicing the discomfort that comes from failure, can be the small steps that impact those resistant to innovation. It is also important to realize that making small changes can be just as important to innovation as big change—and people may be more comfortable with small change. Innovation does not mean launching a huge, untested program to your entire client population; it means developing and testing out new ideas, prototyping elements of a solution, and piloting on a small scale. Transparency and trust in the process may help bring more people along.

PRIORITIZE INNOVATION

Nonprofits (and other institutions) may also face difficulties that come with competing priorities. As nonprofits, we prioritize our mission. We want to spend time, money, and resources devoted to fulfilling that mission. We want to devote resources to serving our population, to working on their issue, and to advocating their desired change. Innovation is sometimes perceived as competing with that priority. How can we divert energy and resources from current work to invest in innovation? How can scarce resources be further portioned off, away from doing the work and toward something unknown?

While this is a significant challenge, it also represents an opportunity. Innovation does not have to be a competing priority. It can be reenvisioned as central to the core priorities. It can bolster the ability to serve the mission and to work toward ameliorating the social problems you are focused on. It can reenergize staff who are burdened with multiple responsibilities. It can serve as professional development, retooling professionals around new concepts for practice. If innovation is integrated and embedded into practice and policy, it can become part of priorities that are already deeply valued. Once priorities are set that align with innovation, it no longer competes with day-to-day work: it becomes that work.

LIVE YOUR MISSION

A primary attribute that makes nonprofits unique is our steadfast focus on a mission that benefits the greater good of individuals, community, society, or the world. Yes, it is the tax structure and the commitment to reinvest excess funds in the mission rather than distribute them to shareholders that actually defines a nonprofit, but it is the focus on this mission that directs all action.

Mission is an opportunity. It is a uniform place of agreement from which everyone related to the organization should share common thinking. It is an implicit and explicit agreement about what you are doing and why you are there. But it is not without challenges. Having a steadfast mission makes it harder to do things or make change, particularly if those activities do not immediately demonstrate a direct connection to the mission. It leads to agreement over the end goal, but gives less guidance on the strategies to get there. Innovation within the nonprofit context must remain true to the mission of the organization. It must utilize the mission as a galvanizing force, but, to do this, the innovation must clearly advance that mission.

GET THE BOARD ON BOARD

A board of directors is responsible for the financial management and governance of an organization. In for-profit boards, this legal responsibility to the shareholders creates a primary focus on financial accountability. In the nonprofit context, the board is responsible for governing the organization so it best meets the community and social needs that the nonprofit was designed to serve. Legally, the responsibility is tied to ensuring oversight over assets and activities that advance the nonprofit's mission, making decisions in the nonprofit's interest, and ensuring that the nonprofit adheres to laws and its mission. While the legal responsibilities are clear, the roles of nonprofit boards move far beyond these basic duties and involve supporting organizational planning, enhancing the organization's public standing, and ensuring adequate resources for the organization to meet its purpose. When it comes to innovation, the board can create barriers or be the strongest ally, so getting the board on board is critical to innovation success.

Board members must come to realize that innovation work is tied to the organization's goals and will help advance the mission. They need to believe that new financial issues will not arise as a result of innovation. Because the board is responsible for choosing and evaluating the chief executive, board members are hopefully in tune with that person's vision of innovation and organizational goals. Getting the board excited about and invested in innovation work early on will solidify their role as champions.

The board can be a critical asset as board members often come from corporate environments where innovation is already part of the organizational DNA. Board members may bring skills that can be harnessed to support innovation activities. Their outside perspective may be critical as you attempt to look at your issue from new angles. Board members may bring legal, financial, business, or marketing expertise to innovation efforts. Leveraging their skills and experiences can give them a stronger stake in the innovation work and a stronger commitment.

AMPLIFY COMMUNITY RELATIONSHIPS

Social sector organizations purposefully maintain collaborations and partnerships. Often, social problem-solving requires the integration of multiple perspectives and assets, leading to natural alliances among service organizations, government, and the private sector. There is a recognition that partnerships between the sectors are critical for solving complex challenges (Moore & Westley 2009; Bendell 2010). Nonprofits already have and can leverage these relationships for innovation.

Nonprofits also bring another important type of relationship to the table: many nonprofits are partnered with the community. Long-lasting community connections, where nonprofits are embedded in and connected to community members and other types of community organizations (i.e., schools, religious institutions, housing, businesses), strengthen the ability to develop and implement new solutions. Social capital becomes a key asset to understand community needs, to create and execute appropriate solutions that the community wants, and to sustain these solutions.

Community partners bring their own expertise to innovation. Valuing this input creates solutions that are more readily integrated into existing institutions and processes. Furthermore, community investment in innovation means a greater likelihood of usage and sustainability. Community members benefit from being part of the collective vision of innovation, both from engagement in the process and from helping create change. Nonprofit organizations often start from the place of having these relationships and shared goals with the community. Leveraging these assets strengthens innovation efforts.

CAPITALIZE ON SOCIAL SECTOR SMARTS

Nonprofit organizations bring people to the innovation table who have a deep-rooted understanding of the complex social problems they wish to address. Expertise, experience, and professional training related to the social problem are tremendous assets as we work toward solutions. The experience of working with the population of interest and in the community that is the target enhances not only the likelihood of developing a workable solution, but also of acceptance and adaptation by that community.

We need to acknowledge and value this expertise but still be open to the idea that we need to learn more. The challenge of our knowledge is that sometimes it takes a different eye or a different way of thinking to develop a new solution. Sometimes we need a fresh view of the situation to get a different result. Innovation efforts need to celebrate and include our social sector expertise, but we also must acknowledge what we do not know.

Innovation efforts can be guided by those with expertise related to problem and population, but they also need to value community perspectives and embrace new ways of thinking. We need to include those with competencies in innovation techniques, but we also need to value nonprofit expertise. We want to include diverse perspectives and unlikely contributors. To get the most out of innovation requires ideation and implementation that leverages our deep wisdom about complex social issues but also acknowledges our blind spots.

CHANGE THE WORLD WITH WHAT YOU HAVE

Nonprofits (actually all social intrapreneurs) need to be mindful that it can be both a blessing and a curse to change the world with what you have. Nonprofits benefit from already having established structures, people, and supports that are in place to help ideate solutions, test prototypes, and implement innovation. They have back office infrastructure to support program development, handle budgetary concerns, and market new ideas. They have established fundraising mechanisms and systems, and policies for implementation. Individuals with varied professional skills may include established communication teams, working committees, volunteers, technological support, or financial experts. Nonprofits also typically have bricks and mortar—they already have buildings and furniture, vehicles, and office supplies. They are equipped with what they need to do their current work.

Nonprofits have institutional structures, infrastructure, and human capital that they bring to innovation. These provide the backbone to do the work, but this may also mean retooling or refocusing. It may mean working around systems that may not be able to integrate innovation, hitting roadblocks where new ideas clash with existing processes, and responding to challenges from those with a tenacious hold on the status quo. Molding or shaping an existing institution may feel more difficult than starting from scratch. But the assets of the organization will prove helpful at different points in the process. For some organizations, the existing infrastructure will provide the people and resources for ideation, for others these will be helpful for execution, and for others these resources will be key for sustainability. Finding the right time to leverage these structures is critical. And when the structures, people, or systems do not work, having the courage to seek alternatives is crucial. Maintain the ability to move away from existing processes and create new ones or to recognize which staff members can be most successful with innovation work. Be prepared to retrain people in a new way of thinking or with new skills necessary to carry out the work. Utilize buy-in at the top level of the organization and the organization's commitment to innovation to remain steadfast to innovation, even when hurdles arise.

Considerations for Innovation in Nonprofits

- *Mission and program fit*: Throughout the innovation process, regular consideration must be given to the alignment of the innovation with the organization's mission and current programming.
- *Monetary considerations*: While the business sector may have particular funding allocated to innovation, nonprofits must consider economic factors of the innovation process as well as financial projections of the innovation itself.
- *Risk and reward*: Innovation at its core is about taking calculated risks. Because nonprofits must balance risk-taking with financial constraints and social responsibility, special attention must be given to maximizing the likelihood of success for the innovation.
- *Competing priorities*: Established nonprofits may struggle with the balance between using time and resources to devote to innovation that take away from established programs.
- *Board of directors*: Existing nonprofits need to be responsive to their board of directors who may be accustomed to traditional systems. Promoting buy-in and integrating the board becomes an important element of innovating from within existing nonprofits.

- *Relationship with the community*: A long-standing commitment, network, and relationship with the community is a significant asset that nonprofits can leverage when generating new solutions.
- *Intimate knowledge of the issue*: Understanding the multifaceted issues facing the community and specific complexities of the social problem is an area where nonprofits excel. This expertise must be utilized to create sustainable impact.
- *Established structure and systems*: Rather than having to start from scratch, established nonprofits have systems and structures in place. Having this structure may facilitate the establishment and sustainability of innovations and should be leveraged as appropriate. Structures that don't work may need to be retooled or abandoned.

IMPLEMENT INNOVATION: THE NONPROFIT INNOVATION MODEL

Nonprofit organizations have a context that both supports and creates challenges for innovation. To capitalize on available resources and overcome these barriers requires a process that is tailored to and specific for nonprofits. There are many reasons why nonprofits have been tentative to engage in innovation work: there are challenges that prevent allocating resources in this direction, and there are factors that resist change. Providing a process that acknowledges these challenges, leverages nonprofits' capacity and resources, and nurtures organizational culture toward positive change creates organizations with the capacity to create and sustain innovations, not once, but over and over again.

The *Nonprofit Innovation Model* (the IN Model; see Figure 2.2) is an innovation process designed to leverage existing resources and support nonprofits through the challenges that come from their environment. It is designed to help nonprofits move beyond the status quo and realize that innovation is not a *competing* priority—it is a *critical and complementary*

FIGURE 2.2: The Nonprofit Innovation Model.

priority. It is designed for testing the waters of risk and creativity without losing sight of organizational mission and priorities. It helps organizations leverage community relationships and harness the skills of the nonprofit board. This model mobilizes existing staff who want to be engaged in the journey and acknowledges the difficulty of change for many within the organization. In the remainder of this chapter, we outline the IN Model, and, in Part II, we provide the tools to put it into action.

The IN Model utilizes four phases to support nonprofits in preparing for, engaging in, and sustaining innovation: (1) *Initiate*, (2) *Investigate*, (3) *Innovate*, and (4) *Integrate*. These phases can be used to support work on individual innovation projects and on transforming the work of the organization as a whole. The four phases are not expected to proceed in a strictly linear fashion, but instead organizations may find their way in and out of the phases throughout a project's life span. *Innovation from within* requires revisiting these steps in a continuous fashion. As innovation is *integrated* into the organization, new opportunities to *initiate* are likely to follow.

INITIATE TO CREATE MOMENTUM

Nonprofits bring skills, resources, and people to the innovation process. They already have staff working on fundraising, programs, and marketing. Nonprofit organizations have a culture that has been established and has guided action. When organizations want to engage in innovation, they have to initiate the process. In the entrepreneurial space, starting innovation is about an individual's passion and his or her ability to garner attention, resources, and support for that idea. In *innovation from within*, starting innovation requires attention to the readiness of organization and the people who will be engaged.

Initiating innovation requires preparing individuals to lead innovation and to be engaged in the process. It is about creating the right culture and providing the tools needed for innovation work. Mostly, initiation is about creating the momentum developing a vision, and building the team for innovation. This phase is designed to ensure that people are inspired. It is a phase used to communicate messaging around the work and around the importance of innovation. Innovation is not a secret. It is to be flaunted, showcased, and celebrated. This phase provides the time to galvanize an organization-wide understanding of the need for innovation and of the importance of the particular efforts being pursued. Each time innovation work commences, there is a need to initiate—to take stock of organizational readiness and prepare for the work of innovation.

INVESTIGATE TO THOROUGHLY UNDERSTAND

Innovation requires examining a problem and understanding its root cause. It becomes necessary to go beyond the negative outcome or social issue that is visible and understand the deep causes or chain of events that has led to this outcome. Nonprofits bring deep expertise to that process. Nonprofit professionals often have an expert understanding of the social problem and bring their experience of the historical complexities of the issue. This expertise needs to be valued, but new knowledge also should be pursued. The most effective social innovations come from looking at a problem from multiple perspectives, from understanding different viewpoints, and from turning the problem on its side. Going right to problem-solving yields traditional solutions. A different, nuanced understanding of an issue can lead to different solutions.

In this phase, use research data, community perspectives, and existing expertise to enhance the understanding of the problem, but also look for new ways to analyze the issue. Taking the time and space for inquiry, gaining a true understanding of the issue, and looking at the issue differently opens the possibility for innovation. Investigation is about getting the facts and looking for truth through emphatic information gathering and asking the right questions. This phase is about searching for the unknown and expanding our current understanding of a given situation, about learning more and more through every part of the exploratory process. It is about asking questions to get multiple perspectives and gathering data from different sources. It is about aligning the problem with the organization's priorities and harnessing the existing knowledge in the organization. Purposeful, hands-on investigation leads us to rethink the problem and approach innovation with an enriched understanding.

INNOVATE TO GENERATE SOLUTIONS

This is when nonprofits work to create new approaches to respond to social problems. This phase is where creativity meets data to create impact. You are able to respond to the problem based on the knowledge amassed during your investigation phase and innovate to find and develop the strongest solution. Ideate solutions, gather suggestions from unlikely contributors, and utilize a full range of resources to support problem-solving. In this phase, multiple players lend suggestions, which leads to prioritizing solutions.

This phase is not just about brainstorming an idea, but about building a prototype or model. Using the prototype for feedback and testing allows early failures to build into later successes. It allows small wins to be the building blocks for large impact. When ideas are quickly and easily tested, participants are less tied to these ideas. People are more comfortable building on each other's ideas and using parts of a solution to build toward the final model. As the solution becomes more established, begin to design a testable version. Organizations continue to rely on their expertise and to leverage the assets they have for development. Redesign is a common element of this phase as solutions are reshaped for viability or improvement. Innovate is the phase during which solutions are suggested then developed and redesigned. It is a repeated process that lends itself to iterations until the solution fully emerges.

INTEGRATE TO IMPLEMENT AND EMBED

After a solution is developed, organizations still have further to go in the process. In the entrepreneurship space, implementation and scale are the primary challenges. When innovating from within, there is an additional layer of challenge and opportunity, one in which the innovation itself is integrated into the organization and innovation is broadly adapted to support future work.

When people innovate from outside of an organizational structure, with a focus on start-up or entrepreneurship, a set of challenges is associated with building new organizational structure and getting resources for sustainability, but there is also a freedom to build that structure and staff to support the innovation developed. Like-minded staff are hired who support the innovation, and processes are built that are in tune with innovation. When innovation happens within an existing organizational structure, that innovation must be integrated.

Embedding the innovation within the organization may take the development of new structures or the hiring of new staff, but it needs to be done in a way that acknowledges existing structures. Bringing the innovation to scale, evaluating it, and continuing to refine it have to be done with an eye on fit within the existing organization. Rather than favoring the new, nonprofits need to be cognizant of how the new program, project, or activity supports what is already happening. They must create opportunities for other staff to be a part of the innovation and to know what is going on. Even when a new structure is established (e.g., if the new innovation involves building a separate profit-generating entity), existing staff need to be aware of its purpose and its distinction.

Each innovation project represents a learning opportunity, a chance for the organization to grow and to embed innovation deeper into its core. Integrating is about making this happen. Innovation is always about change, but it is critical that the change becomes part of the organization. John Kotter wrote in *Leading Change* (1996) that "change sticks only when it becomes 'the way we do things around here,' when it seeps into the very bloodstream of the work unit or corporate body."

The *Integrate* phase is about seeding that organizational change. Integration is about building a better, stronger organization; one that can innovate not just with this one project, but one that is set up to innovate over and over again. It is about creating an organization that can respond to new challenges with ease and can leverage new tools as they are developed.

As the *Integrate* phase concludes, new challenges will no doubt arise that lead the organization to initiate new innovation cycles. Each time this happens, the organization is stronger and more poised for the work, but it still needs to commit to each part of the process. The IN Model helps nonprofits organize each time this happens and reevaluate what needs to be done. There will always be new challenges, but this process helps create nonprofits that are ready to meet them. And using this momentum creates different nonprofit organizations—ones that are truly innovative.

REFLECTION FOR CLAIMING THE NONPROFIT ROLE IN INNOVATION

1. Reflect on the need for innovation in a social problem area that concerns you. Do any of the factors discussed in the first part of the chapter apply?
2. Reflect on your commitment to nonprofit engagement in social innovation. What do you see as opportunities and challenges?

3. The IN Model is a process for engaging in innovation work. Does the process seem workable? Could you imagine going through the steps? Where might you have difficulty?

MAIN POINTS FOR CLAIMING THE NONPROFIT ROLE IN INNOVATION

- Today's nonprofits must be innovative to respond to a changing context. Existing social problems, a competitive marketplace, declining resources, eroding sectoral boundaries, globalization, and the ubiquity of technology demand that nonprofits respond to social problems in new ways.
- Nonprofits have to acknowledge and respond to challenges related to money, naysayers, and competing priorities. These can be managed and used as advantages.
- A steadfast focus on mission is an asset that nonprofits can use to support innovation.
- Nonprofits need to recognize the benefit of different types of capital—human capital, community relationships, social sector knowledge, board assets, and infrastructure—for supporting innovation.
- The IN Model outlines the process for *innovation from within* nonprofits:
  - *Initiate* to create momentum within your organization and mobilize staff as innovators.
  - *Investigate* to thoroughly understand the issue and look at it in different ways.
  - *Innovate* to generate solutions and develop a testable prototype.
  - *Integrate* to implement and embed innovation in the organizational context and to support innovation not once, but over and over again.

CHAPTER 3

CULTIVATE INNOVATIVE NONPROFITS

Doing innovation work requires the right people, tools, and mindset; innovative organizations are made not born.

> **Get ready to ...**
> 1. Build the people power for innovation through leaders, teams, and meaningful partners.
> 2. Cultivate the right skills and tools for innovation.
> 3. Galvanize thinking that allows creativity to flourish and innovation to emerge.

For nonprofits to be ready for innovation requires examining literature and practice that supports this aim. We often hear stories of successful innovations that have had tremendous impact on a specific social issue or of innovators who started with an idea and saw it to fruition. But we don't often talk about what it took to get there. How and why do some innovations make it? How did it go from idea to success? What happened to the failures? While the popular images do not highlight this black box, there is a lot of research that does unpack successful innovation. Borrowing on this research and our past work, we outline the frameworks, practice, and process that support the creation of successful innovations. Working with hundreds of nonprofit leaders, we have seen the pitfalls and possibilities of innovation. We have seen game-changing ideas get developed only to sit on a shelf and be underutilized. We have worked with agencies that have piloted tremendous programs and were unable to scale. And we have seen groups of intrapreneurs work tirelessly for change only to face resistance from the larger organization. But we have also seen successes that have fully developed, tested, launched, and integrated innovation into the very core of an existing agency. Lessons from these successes and failures, data from our own research, and information from the existing literature provide insight into what it takes to engage in innovation work. What elements are critical prior to going through an innovation process? What do you need in place to be ready to use the Nonprofit Innovation (IN) Model? How can we orient ourselves differently so our processes, solutions, outcomes, and impact are creative and fresh?

We need frameworks and tools to be inspired, to orient (or reorient) ourselves toward innovation, and to be ready to lead others. Having specific frameworks and tools also creates opportunities for education and training and for retooling when success is elusive. If we want to reframe our understanding of innovation from a magical process that spontaneously occurs to one we can work toward, we must rely on frameworks to guide us. We must understand what it takes to have the capacity for innovation and consciously work to promote it. This chapter provides the frameworks and tools to set up the right conditions for innovation.

The Right Conditions for Innovation

- People
  - Leaders for change
  - Powerful teams
  - Meaningful partners
- Tools
  - Expansive communication
  - Design thinking
  - Technology
- Mindset
  - Beginner's mindset
  - Social commitment
  - Empathy
  - Tolerance for failure
  - Planfulness

DEVELOP PERSONNEL FOR INNOVATION: READY THE LEADERS, READY THE TEAM

Building innovation capacity at the organizational level relies on leveraging existing talents and building new strengths. People form the basis of institutions and determine their appetite and aptitude for change. Organizations that have the right leaders, foster the power of teams, and cultivate critical partnerships are better positioned for the innovation trajectory.

LEAD FOR CHANGE

There is a tremendous amount of literature connecting leadership to change in organizations. Leaders set the context, create the vision for the future, and establish the culture that embraces innovation. The leader is critical to stimulating and sustaining creativity, supporting risk-taking and experimentation, and catalyzing action. Leaders shape the organizational culture and climate to be one that lives innovation to the core.

The type of leaders who imbue innovation share similar characteristics like ...

- Vision for the future, with attention paid to the possible contexts of tomorrow.
- Shared leadership style that motivates and supports others.
- Capacity to lead by example with their own innovation efforts.
- Ability to catalyze action, leverage collective work, and harness individual creativity.
- Willingness to provide the necessary resources and attention for experimentation and new ideas.
- Steadfast commitment to communicating about innovation and its centrality to agency mission.
- Support for creativity, risk-taking, and experimentation.
- Acceptance of those who challenge the status quo and traditional processes.
- Ability to evaluate new initiatives and use failures as learning opportunities.
- Commitment to and talent with engaging key stakeholders and their board.

Osterwalder reminds us that "the C-suite needs a chief entrepreneur," a person whose visionary leadership on innovation, growth, and experimentation sits at the highest level of an organization (Osterwalder 2015). Because leaders drive the culture of organizations, they have the opportunity to shape the environment toward innovation. Moreover, because leaders exist within all levels of a nonprofit, it is vital that leadership skills for innovation be fostered among leaders of all levels—from the executive director to the lead case manager and every decision-maker in between.

NURTURE THE POWER OF TEAMS

There is a widely misguided notion that innovation is somehow the brainchild of an individual working in isolation. Instead, history and experience demonstrate that, in fact, innovation is often spurred and cultivated through the use of purposeful teams. Many discoveries have been done in groups. Take, for example, the famous Thomas Edison Menlo Park Laboratory. Edison brought together people from all over the world with vastly different skills, including glassblowers, clockmakers, carpenters, scientists, and mathematicians. These teams working in collaboration built on the individual capacity of the members, learned from their context, worked to develop coherence by working through disagreement, and dealt adeptly with the complexities of the market (Miller Caldicott 2012). This purposeful team approach led to discoveries that went far beyond individual genius. Fischer and Boynton contend that virtuoso teams, purposefully convened for important projects and utilizing elite experts in intimate, intense work conditions create extraordinary results (Boynton & Fisher 2005).

Teams play the powerful role of allowing different types of creativity to emerge and different conversations to be explored. They allow for quick idea exchange and building momentum. This feeding off of each other's ideas stimulates and encourages original thought. Teams can take advantage of diverse perspectives by having members that represent different genders, ethnicities, educational backgrounds, experiences, and organizational roles. Adding *unlikely suspects*, or people who might not typically be involved in innovation or in the specific project area, leads to creative discussion. Having people with a variety of perspectives encourages members to think differently. Furthermore, teams that capture the diversity of talent allow a new set of ideas to emerge.

Organizations that purposefully build for innovation create teams that:

- Capture the diversity of talent.
- Recognize the power of including unlikely suspects.
- Give real power and autonomy to teams to support action and decision-making.
- Prepare team members so they have the competencies needed to be successful.
- Engage teams in all aspects of innovation from ideation and development to implementation and sustainability.
- Recognize that different teams are needed for different purposes.
- Meaningfully stimulate and leverage team creativity.

Teams also play an important role as we consider the diffusion and adoption of innovation. While programs often fail due to employee resistance, teams allow for greater investment across an organization, so there are more allies for implementation and supporters when challenges arise. When innovation is readily understood and championed by multiple people at the organization, there is a greater likelihood of success and sustainability.

ENGAGE MEANINGFUL PARTNERS

Innovation often draws on the talents and resources of meaningful partnerships. Complex problems are often best solved by working across the organization and across the sector. They often require strategic alignment and investment from nonprofits, business, and government. Multisector collaboration creates greater investment and higher chances of sustainability. This is not to say that all innovation requires established collaboration or formal relationships, but rather that organizations that have the right conditions for innovation are open to beginning or have established meaningful partnerships.

Examples from the Field

Innovate United is a social innovation initiative led by the United Way of the Greater Triangle in North Carolina. The project brings together intrapreneurs, entrepreneurs, funders, for-profits, and nonprofits to develop innovative solutions to issues related to low-income families in the region. Through social innovation challenges and a pitch competition, the project brings together partners from across the region to develop and fund innovative solutions.

The complexity of today's issues often goes beyond the capacity of a single organization. Problems simultaneously demand expertise from across disciplines and often across sectors. Living Cities (livingcities.org) brings together 22 foundations and financial institutions to support building new approaches to support low-income people in urban environments. But what is unique about this cross-city collaboration is that it engages not only the funding community, but also includes academic, nonprofit, and government partners. Through this broad collaboration, they build urban practice that has the resources and commitment to be effective and sustainable.

Nonprofits need to think about how to develop and manage these types of collaborative relationships. Continually scanning the environment for these partnerships prepares the agency to be ready to seize opportunities that arise. And then, when they arise, engaging an active set of diverse partners forces the organization to examine problems holistically and to consider the widest range of possible solutions.

Relationships with for-profit partners may involve skill-sharing, branding, and resources. Partnerships with other nonprofits may open the possibility to collaboration, new clients, new locations, or expanded skill sets. Public partnerships pave the way for service provision and policy change. Building and maintaining relationships with organizations that share mission, have complementary skills, or support expanded services helps drive and sustain innovation.

Meaningful partnerships are not limited to relationships with other organizations. They also include active relationships with community members and community groups. These community alliances can support the development and adaptation of innovation. Establishing these partnerships early and shepherding them through the innovation process leads to a greater stake in the innovation. It allows resistance to be exposed early on, before the investment is too great, and allows problems to be fixed before they become entrenched in the process or the outcome. Community becomes a strong ally, particularly as we attempt to do things differently. With this allyship, we are more likely to develop solutions based on problems as defined by the community's lived experience and not by our perception of the problem, which can often overlook key elements.

> **Organizations that leverage relationships for successful innovation:**
>
> - Establish relationships with a diverse set of partners that share similar perspectives or complementary skills.
> - Engage partnerships across the for-profit, nonprofit, and public sectors.
> - Consider partnerships that are focused on specific projects and longer term relationships.
> - Reflect on how partnerships serve your organization.
> - Include community groups or alliances as potential partners for collaboration.
> - Identify problems and solutions *with* the community rather than *for* the community.

Organizations that build strong relationships with other organizations and the community have the flexibility to leverage these relationships within and across projects. The more people who are invested in a project, the greater chance for implementation and sustainability. But these organizations also possess a nimbleness that dictates how they move into and out of relationships. They are able to sustain long-term relationships that are meaningful, but also to form and reform relationships as needed. They are able to reconsider relationships with funders and fluidly move across roles. They are able to recognize the strengths and capacities of others but maintain an eye on their own capacities and how they are being utilized. Organizations that are ready for innovation utilize people power to their capacity. They have leaders who drive process, teams who are able to innovate and implement, and partnerships that support their work. They are open to shared work and shared visioning but have a steadfast commitment to their own clear message.

BUILD CAPACITY FOR SUCCESS: COMMUNICATION, DESIGN THINKING, AND TECHNOLOGY

Social innovation requires the right personnel, but also appropriate tools and skills. Tools that support communication, design thinking, and technology provide supports that guide innovation work. Some of these tools may already exist at your organization, while others can be learned and cultivated to support innovation activities.

> **Organizations with the necessary tools for innovation:**
>
> - Cultivate multiple communication tools that allow conversation across language, culture, and ability.
> - Nurture creativity with tools for drawing, art, and media.
> - Use the basics of design thinking and apply it their environment.

- Integrate technology into the process to stimulate new ways of thinking and open the potential for new solutions.
- Encourage people to have open minds.
- Use social interactions as the driver for success.
- Capitalize on the power of technology as a tool to measure social impact.
- Promote empathy.
- Experiment. Experiment. Experiment.
- Purposefully create time, space, and structures for innovation.

COMMUNICATE WITH EASE

Perhaps the most fundamental tool to developing an environment for innovation is creating multiple avenues for communication. Communication tools open up the potential for work across culture and language, but also for different interpretations of the problem and therefore different solutions. Communication tools support creative outlets that shift conversations and open new paradigms. For nonprofit organizations, learning how to communicate more effectively with and across diverse ability, language, and culture is critical. Cultural humility suggests a need to understand things from the perspective of those you engage with. The focus on populations across socioeconomic status and across disability requires attention to engaging multiple communication tools that allow the voice of diverse perspectives.

The integration of nonverbal tools in nonprofit work, including drawings, photos, and videos, promote inclusive engagement and remove barriers for many. Nontraditional sources of input, including allowing participants to engage in poetry writing, newspaper development, blogging, or social media, allows different information to be shared. Storytelling allows powerful narratives to be shared, others to be inspired, and new information to be extracted. When you open the possibility for new avenues of communication, you encourage the possibility that fresh ideas will emerge. You reduce some common communication barriers, like the fear of speaking out in a large group or a failure to appeal to learners of all kinds—visual, auditory, and kinesthetic. When you utilize the same tools that you always have, you are likely to get the same output. When you run meetings with the same conversations or collect data with the same interview formats, you are likely to draw out the same information. But new ways of collecting and sharing information open the flow of information and the possibility for new conversations.

Different types of communication also lead to creativity. As we speak about creativity, we are not promoting the development of a masterpiece, but rather the unleashing of input from a variety of means. It may be drawings or photographs or videos. People remember drawings more than words, and visual displays are open to different interpretation. These interpretations spark greater exploration and symbolism than do words. This is not about being an artist or demonstrating superior graphic design. It is about using a new lens to approach the topic. Everyone has these skills; it's a matter of tapping into creativity or artistry and letting these new communication tools guide us.

Different methods of communication also allow us to hear from those who may not have the opportunity to contribute otherwise. Adding new tools that allow for nonverbal or alternative communication is meant to be inclusive. It puts people on a new playing field, one that is not dominated by the outspoken, and it allows people to share in a different way. The leader of the organization and the direct service worker can be on the same page in terms of the drawing skills they contribute. Community groups who have historically been marginalized or less often heard can participate in a process in which they feel more comfortable and capable of contributing equally. Field work across location, language, culture, and immigration experience becomes more open to hearing different voices. Those with lower educational or reading levels are able to actively contribute and share their voice as input. Young people who have grown up in a world of digital images and multimedia may prefer to express themselves in ways other than words. We must consider our audience and utilize diverse skill sets to promote participation.

Different methods of communication also offer new opportunities for listening. They provide new spaces for pause and silence. The silence that comes while another person is drawing or the break you have to take when thinking about how to express yourself nonverbally creates powerful disruptions in thought that can trigger new thoughts to emerge. Sometimes it is the space that opens the mind to possibility. Diversifying communication strategies builds in these spaces because we are less adept at using these tools, and therefore we take our time.

Having a fluency and comfort with using a variety of communication tools opens up the greatest possibility for creativity and diversity. It is not about learning another language or adopting a particular strategy, but instead about being versed in a variety of tools that allow for new communication patterns to emerge.

UNDERSTAND DESIGN THINKING

As we build capacity for innovation in the nonprofit sector, we maintain attention on innovation work happening in different fields. While not a new concept, the management and design fields have been using design thinking as a strategy and process to stimulate innovation (Brown 2009). Coined by David Kelley, founder of IDEO, *design thinking* involves a set of principles used to solve complex problems. It generally involves expanded strategies for understanding the problem, generating solutions, and engaging in testing. Design thinking draws heavily on the use of multiple materials to make problem assessment and solution generation visible and tangle processes.

Brown suggests design thinking as three overlapping steps that include inspiration to recognize and understand the problem, ideation to develop solutions, and implementation to move from development to application. Visual activities and prototyping solutions are key activities of the process.

Design thinking also takes a human-centered approach, putting the experiences of the people who may become the end user of the solution at the center of the process. The focus on the user leads us to ask for the user's perspective at each step in the design process:

1. How the user would see the problem
2. How the user would interact with the product or service
3. What motivates the user
4. How the user would experience the solution

The user's needs are at the forefront of each step in the process. Stimulating innovation in the nonprofit sector borrows on these tools and adapts the approach to fit the context. For nonprofits, there may be an implicit assumption that we lack resources to engage in testing and rapid redesign, that risk aversion limits the potential for experimentation, or that our problems are simply too large to use the design thinking approach to act first. But many in the sector already do testing and refinement in work with individual clients or on specific issues. Most work to include end-user perspectives and client input. Where design thinking extends the client-centered perspective is by actively engaging the user and his or her perspectives throughout the steps in a process.

Furthermore, design thinking guides a specific set of strategies to support (1) understanding the problem to be addressed, (2) generating solutions, and (3) engaging in testing. Design thinking implores the organization to physically get out and understand the problem at hand; to generate diverse and plentiful ideas (before jumping to solutions); to prototype and reiterate fast, low-cost representations of the solution; and to get significant feedback to help with reprototyping. Different from the traditional nonprofit "pilot" program, which can take significant resources and investment before roll-out, prototyping asks the designer to develop representations of ideas and to get feedback and do testing before developing the fully functional idea. Nonprofits can and should learn from these approaches to support user input, greater experimentation, and more acceptance of feedback. From design thinking, we can borrow processes and tools to be incorporated into the nonprofit context.

INFUSE TECHNOLOGY WHEN POSSIBLE

Information and communication technology (ICT) has the transformational power to create connections, open access, and spark new solutions in the social sector. An inextricable link exists between technology and innovation. Technology and innovation operate within a reciprocal relationship, with technology driving innovation in some cases and innovation expanding technology use or application in others. ICT has the potential to be the innovation itself or to encourage the development of non–tech-based solutions. Using technology also creates a different mindset, often encouraging a range of thoughts and solutions that otherwise would not have been possible. It becomes a catalyst for creativity, it may open up solution generation to a wider set of people (think social media crowdsourcing or virtual team approaches), and it paves the way to tech-based solutions. Technology can also be used to elicit feedback and input on developed designs.

Nonprofits have often been slower in the engagement of technologies than their for-profit counterparts, a fact often driven by the lack of resources, expertise, time, and ability for experimentation. Nonprofit agencies that do build capacity for technology, whether in service, administrative, or process functions, are more apt to innovate. Integrating technology into different organizational, communication, service delivery, evaluation, and operations functions at the organization unleashes creativity and the emergence of new ideas.

As we look into the next 20 years of nonprofit practice, we are enticed by the promise of new technologies that support population outcomes, improve efficiency, and track the efficacy of our programs. There are specific technologies related to mobile technology, social media, gaming, robotics, and wearable technologies that have garnered interest for their potential to transform the social sector (Berzin, Singer, & Chan 2015). But it is not the game of "playing catch up," trying to forever learn new technology that matters. It is the paradigm shift in which nonprofits approach technology as an imperative that will drive innovation and further our mission. It is a shift to an active and aggressive role in the adoption and development of technologies that are consistent with nonprofit goals. It is the growth in a more active role in developing, adapting, and implementing a wider set of ICTs to serve the sector.

Technology-based tools can be brought into the innovation process at every step. Tools can be used for enhancing communication, involving a greater set of participants, collecting different sources of data, piloting, prototyping, and implementation. Digitally based strategies have the opportunity to engage a wider set of participants in each part of the process. Technology also shifts the type of data that can be collected to include continuous feedback, biomarkers, and GPS data. From an output perspective, ICT creates new solution possibilities that involve mobile applications, gaming, robotics, and social media. Developing, integrating, and using technology-based tools paves the way for other innovations to take hold.

To work with technology requires attention to gaps in technology skills and knowledge in the sector. Training that equips staff with knowledge of the fundamentals of technology and prepares them to incorporate technology effectively is critical. Incorporating technology into other staff development opportunities also supports adoption. Rather than decontextualizing technology as simply a discrete set of technical skills, it supports the development of staff members who are technology-literate. This integrated approach will prepare organizations to most readily use and access technology as needed.

THINK LIKE AN INNOVATOR: ADOPT A MINDSET FOR INTRAPRENEURSHIP

Innovation requires not only tools and people, but also changing paradigms. Developing an organization that is ready to engage in innovation work involves preparing people to think like innovators. Innovators are not just risk-takers who blindly go after change: they are individuals who purposefully seek out experimentation and learn from their work. Innovators know how to learn from others, embrace creativity, and celebrate diversity. Actively working toward adapting an innovator's mindset comes with practice and purpose.

ADOPT A BEGINNER'S MINDSET

Thinking like an innovator keeps the mind open to creativity and available to new ideas. Humility starts us down that path. When we adopt a beginner's mindset, we are open to different solutions and able to learn. *Beginner's mind* is a Buddhist concept that guides us to view every moment as an opportunity to learn something new and view something in a completely different way (Suzuki 2006). As Zen Master Shuer Shunryu reminds us "In the beginner's mind there are many possibilities, but in the expert's there are few." It encourages you to set preconceived notions aside and approach each situation as a new experience. If we approach problem-solving from this perspective, it allows us to take each step without worrying about or rushing toward the endpoint. Keeping an open mind leaves room for intuition without getting caught up in prejudging and predetermining the outcome. A beginner's mindset encourages the use of experience but also the letting go of being an expert. It encourages inquiry and living in the moment to gather new information about the situation or experience. Through this approach, we open our minds to different ways of viewing the problem at hand and the broadest range of possible solutions.

REMEMBER "SOCIAL"

In considering social innovation success, it becomes imperative to embed the "social" in all that we do. Innovators understand the importance of social ties and relationships. Some definitions of social innovation include new social relationships as a necessary component while others acknowledge the tremendous potential of within- and cross-sector partnerships for doing transformative work (The Young Foundation 2012). As we consider the "social" in social innovation, we consider a new idea to be social embeddedness. *Social embeddedness* refers to a dual understanding of the word "social," one that pertains to our purpose and one that describes our interaction.

Social reminds us of the reason for innovation work undertaken in this context. It refers to the goals to ameliorate social problems and enhance social justice. Equity in communities and enhancing the lives of others remains the "true north" of our work and trumps issues in funding and design. Different from other sectors that take on innovation work, nonprofit innovation is guided by an unwavering commitment to address social problems. Therefore, each step in our process must be viewed through the lens of its impact on individuals, communities, and society. The outcomes we seek to achieve must be viewed from the lens of inherent dignity and respect of the persons we wish to serve.

As critical as the lens of social justice is to our work, the term "social" also directs us with our process. Inherently, innovation is a process that demands interaction. It is rarely pursued in isolation and it gains strength from connection. We pursue social innovation recognizing that our ability to generate ideas is strengthened when we draw from multiple perspectives. Interacting and engaging with community, peers, leaders, and experts strengthens the innovator's ability to develop, implement, and sustain the best possible solutions. Drawing on diverse collective perspectives only strengthens this approach. Innovation requires a mindset that explores and leverages social embeddedness to maintain the mission and make the most of social context.

OPEN YOUR EYES TO OTHERS

Innovation must start with empathy as a critical element for reciprocal partnerships and authentic solidarity with marginalized groups of people. Being aware of other perspectives and trying to understand the world through a different lens sheds light on the human condition, making us better able to solve complex problems. Having the capacity for empathy allows you leave behind preconceived notions and stereotypes that often fall short of the true experience. Empathy allows us to more deeply understand the problems we seek to address and create solutions that will be more readily accepted by those in need.

The strength of a social service orientation is training in and appreciation for understanding the perspective of others. This extends our capacity to understand another person's condition from their unique perspective and to embolden our attention to diversity in our work. When this is coupled with a beginner's mindset, we allow ourselves to appreciate that while we have plenty of cultural insight on the communities with which we work, there is still plenty more to learn and understand.

Cultural sensitivity has deep roots in the social sector and it enables professionals (and systems) to work cross-culturally. Innovation, too, needs this perspective. To create transformative programs, policies, and products requires attention to diverse perspectives and knowledge of the cultures in which we seek to intervene. Deeper attention to culture allows a more nuanced understanding of social problems and the structural sources of social, economic, and environmental injustice. Furthermore, the adoption of developed interventions and their shared ownership by the community requires the kind of partnership that comes only through culturally competent work.

BE WILLING TO TRY, OPEN TO FAILURE

Innovation is predicated on the foundation of experimentation. You cannot be innovative if you do not try new things. But trying is often met with failure—and being open and willing to accept failure and learn from it is a key component of an innovation mindset. Engaging in practice to experiment with new ideas and make rapid change allows people to "try-on" failure. Not all ideas are going to be good ones, but building on failures and learning from them can be the foundation for the solution. From an iterative process of trial, failure, adaptation, and trial again comes the opportunity to develop and improve upon potential solutions. But accepting failure is not innate or a cultural norm. We are guided by a penchant for success, and we celebrate when we get the answer right. We avoid failure and cover up mistakes because we assume mistakes show weakness. But innovation requires openness to trial and a comfort with error. It begs an acceptance of uncertainty and an opportunity to explore without concern for failure. Experimentation allows more chances for creative solutions. Early failure allows more opportunities for improvement and more opportunities to learn from the experience. Iterative approaches that include opportunities for feedback allow you to learn from failure and to build on your ideas. Innovation in nonprofits requires this commitment to experimentation and openness to failure.

Although innovation is about experimentation, it is not about leaving things up to chance. It is about planning with purpose and learning from mistakes. In innovation, we purposefully integrate the steps of the process with the future work. We could simply wait for innovation to occur, or we can purposefully and mindfully create opportunities and spaces for innovation to occur. To think like an innovator means paying attention to and creating these opportunities. It means growing (and flexing) the innovation muscles of the staff and embedding innovation practices and processes into the organization. The Innovation Audit (see Chapter 4) helps organizations document their strengths in innovation and where they have room for growth. This can be used as a starting point to plan for innovation and measure progress in how well the agency embraces innovation.

Companies like Warby Parker and Toyota who made the Fast Company Top 50 Most Innovative Companies List in 2015 (Chafkin 2015) embed innovation in their work (Blumenthal 2016). Innovative organizations in the social sector, like UTEC, purposefully amplify a culture and capacity around innovation. Other nonprofits need to build that same type of support and structure for innovation while maintaining a steadfast focus on social impact. *Innovation from within* is about deliberately building those processes.

Examples from the Field

Toyota embeds innovation into their work through processes and practice. Beliefs like *kaizen* (continuous improvement) and *genchi genbutsu* (go out and see) are driven into their work. When designing a new truck, designers visited truck graveyards in Michigan to see the evolution of the industry and visited different users in different circumstances to understand their needs. On their website, innovation is front and center on the navigation pane, second only to showroom, emphasizing this commitment (toyota-global.com).

UTEC builds innovation into every part of its organization to support proven-risk youth in their drive for social and economic success. They have dedicated innovation personnel, including a Chief Innovation Officer, and have entrenched cultural practices around innovation for all employees. They use multiple intervention strategies including five social enterprises. Their building is LEED Platinum Certified and contains messages of innovation on the walls (utec-lowell.org).

Warby Parker asks employees for "innovation ideas"; purposefully creates physical spaces for games and natural interactions to occur; schedules Demo Days for departments to demonstrate their newest work; hosts Hackathons to foster intensive, quick-paced collaboration opportunities; and values innovation through the integration of staff ideas into how the company operates (warbyparker.com).

An organization with the right conditions for innovation intentionally sets out to create the context. Perhaps some of the necessary elements are already in place, but others need to be developed and cultivated. Creating the condition for innovation is about developing the right people, building or integrating the right tools, and encouraging the right mindset.

REFLECTION FOR CULTIVATING INNOVATIVE NONPROFITS

1. Consider a nonprofit where you work or to which you are connected. Does that organization have the right human capital to engage in innovation work? Are there strengths or weak spots among leadership, individuals, or partners?
2. Brainstorm 10 ways you can communicate an idea. Be broad and creative.
3. Technology is both a method and an outcome. Explore a problem in your work and how technology could be used as both part of the process and part of the solution.
4. Contemplate your own "innovation mindset." How closely does your mindset align with the elements of *thinking like an innovator*? How might you retool for new thinking?

MAIN POINTS FOR CULTIVATING INNOVATIVE NONPROFITS

- Leaders do not need to wait for innovation to emerge. It is something you can purposefully build the capacity and skills for.
- Innovation does not just happen. It requires planning, consideration, and purpose. Through leadership, the power of teams, and the establishment of meaningful partnerships, we begin to develop the right conditions for social innovation.
- Broad communication tools are critical to developing and implementing innovation.
- Borrowed from outside the nonprofit sector, design thinking processes become powerful supports for innovation to emerge.
- There is a complex entanglement of innovation and technology. Technology creates the conditions and potential for innovation while simultaneously opening a wider set of solutions.
- Innovation is about thinking like an innovator and building the capacity for others in your organization to think in the same way. Working with others and engaging through interaction are critical to developing and implementing innovation.
- Having a beginner's mindset and learning from failure are key parts of the experimentation and innovation process.
- In social innovation, social justice and social impact are our true north.

INNOVATION IN ACTION

CATALYZE THEORY INTO ACTION

As leaders in social justice, we are compelled to uncover and understand inequities and to generate opportunities for social transformation. Part I described numerous vehicles beyond traditional interventions that help stimulate social change. Part II puts you in the driver's seat of our process for social innovation so that you and your organization can lead the way for innovation in the nonprofit field. Utilizing the Nonprofit Innovation Model (IN Model; see Figure 2.1) introduced in Part I, we specify the ingredients to foster innovation in the workplace, define the framework for contextualizing a social issue, develop a response to the challenge, and incorporate change into the organization.

The IN Model helps you and your innovation team create opportunities within problems. The process was built by integrating the best of innovation from the nonprofit sector with learning from other sectors, adapted and adjusted to fit our context. It was tested with agencies and nonprofit leaders both locally and globally, addressing a range of social issue areas and problems. Developing the process was iterative, building on what we learned along the way and using feedback for refinement. Nonprofit agencies approached the process with problems ranging from Alzheimer's treatment to charter school metrics to youth violence to family homelessness to pollution and urban transportation. Solutions ranged from mobile technology to gaming to program development to policy change. Nonprofit leaders struggled with finding time and space for innovation, but found allies among board members, beneficiaries, and community partners. Doing innovation projects created ambassadors for innovation in the agencies and in some cases led to new organizational processes and structures (e.g., prototyping sessions, an innovation idea box, an innovation review process,

FIGURE P2.1: Nonprofit IN Model

and innovation competitions). As our process developed, core concepts introduced in Chapter 3 kept reemerging as central to the process. The IN Model relies heavily on the power of teams, uses creative communication strategies, employs design thinking, requires a beginner's mindset, allows failure and reiteration, integrates diversity and cultural relevance, relies on social embeddedness, and exploits empathy as a critical tool for achieving innovation that is committed to social justice.

Important Terms for Social Innovation Work

Design thinking is a human-centered design process that uses overlapping phases to understand a problem, ideate and test solutions, and implement results.

Beginner's mindset is a way to approach each situation as a new experience, with an open mind and no predetermined outcome.

Empathy is the ability to understand others in an authentic and reciprocal way.

Social embeddedness emphasizes the word "social" as a guide for both our outcomes as they relate to alleviating social problems and our process as it requires interaction.

In Part I, you, the individual, were exposed to new concepts and frameworks to understand innovation and its application in the nonprofit context. Now, expanding out to the organizational level, you and your innovation team will use this section to *Initiate, Investigate, Innovate*, and *Integrate* innovation into your nonprofit. This process is purposefully participatory, fast-paced, and iterative. We concern ourselves with thinking big and trying ideas out on a small scale. We embrace the need for trying, failing, learning, and trying again. We understand the value of team building and idea sharing. And we are rooted in our commitment to the community and our intimate understanding of the social issues we tackle.

APPLY AND ADAPT THE IN MODEL

The nonprofit context is a nuanced environment. As we outlined in Part I, we can't expect that an approach from another sector can be directly applied to nonprofits. Existing nonprofits have specific considerations when innovating, such as managing overhead costs, responding to an existing board of directors, risk aversion, and their long-standing relationship with the community—all of which must be considered and leveraged. This is why *Innovation from within* nonprofits requires a social innovation process that is tailored to the unique circumstances in which we exist. It must challenge nonprofit leaders to consider and act within these conditions, and it must do so at every step of the way. The IN Model guides you through that process.

The four phases of the IN Model, *Initiate, Investigate, Innovate,* and *Integrate,* are all practical, activity-based sections that will guide your team from start to finish. The first chapter of Part II gives you guidance, examples, and practical activities for you to *Initiate* innovation within your agency by developing a culture of innovation. Because many nonprofits are new to social innovation processes, exposing the staff to its core principles and the rich possibilities that social innovation offers will be key prior to launching your first social innovation project. In the next phase of the IN Model, *Investigate,* your innovation team will identify an issue to address and engage in several hands-on strategies to deeply understand the issue inside and out. This will serve as an essential foundation for the *Innovate* phase, in which your team will ideate the (im)possible and develop promising solutions to the identified issue. Following a period of idea development, your team will also implement alpha and beta tests of your innovation, where you can add, subtract, rethink, or expand your innovation based on the feedback systems you design. Once your team has agreed to move your innovation forward, you will enter the final stage of the innovation process, *Integrate.* Here, you will take steps to weave innovation into your nonprofit by leveraging your organization's resources and existing strengths. By the end of the process, you will have generated both enthusiasm and capacity in your organization to launch innovations not just once, but over and over again.

These phases help you build solutions, but they move beyond one project toward creating a new culture of innovation. They are designed to purposefully support you and a team of fellow innovators as you navigate the complexities of innovating from within. Throughout your innovation process, you and your team will strengthen your likelihood for success by addressing questions such as "How does this idea align with the mission of our organization?" "How can we enhance input from our stakeholders?" and "How can we engage the executive leadership and board of directors in our innovation process?" Regularly assessing these and other questions is imperative for the success of new initiatives.

An innovation with little staff buy-in has a greater likelihood of falling by the way-side than one that has mindfully integrated staff and stakeholders from the beginning. If you have assessed for mission fit along the way, your innovation is likely to better complement your existing programs and qualify under similar funding sources for expansion. It is also important to pay attention to the balance between innovation, other tasks, and competing priorities, and leveraging existing organizational resources makes it possible. The IN Model will allow you to keep your eye on the larger picture while paying attention to the smaller details that will ensure success along the way.

This part of the book guides you through the steps to *Initiate* a culture of innovation, *Investigate* to understand the issues your organization is facing, *Innovate* to develop and test new solutions, and *Integrate* successful ideas into your nonprofit. The steps outlined are not concretely linear, but rather they are in a loosely sequential order that has been shown to be effective when implemented in nonprofits. Sometimes—often—you and your innovation team will be required to pause, retrace some steps, or jump forward a bit. Mix and match the suggested guidelines as it makes sense for your organization.

Keep in mind that these are merely guidelines. Some parts will be particularly relevant to your organization, while other sections may not necessarily apply due to the unique circumstances of your nonprofit. Feel free to pick and choose activities accordingly. If you don't currently have the capacity at your organization to implement the innovation process in its entirety, use select activities to facilitate creative brainstorming sessions or to understand some difficult problems your agency might be facing. Use this book to open a conversation or stimulate dialogue with staff and board members about the infinite opportunities to engage in innovation and social impact. As always, when it's possible to tailor any strategy to better fit your organization, please do so—make this process your own!

Let's innovate!

CHAPTER 4

INITIATE

$\mathcal{C}$hapter 4 establishes an innovation mindset within your agency to build the right momentum and spark creativity.

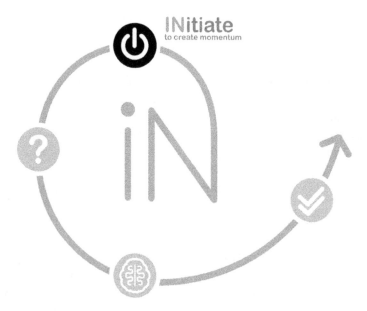

FIGURE 4.1: Initiate model.

Get ready to ...

1. Create a vision for long-term innovation.
2. Develop and implement strategies for getting your organization on board with innovation.
3. Recruit and prepare your innovation team members.

Successfully implementing innovation is all about readiness. It is about having the *right leadership* to support innovation, the *right staff* to develop ideas and implement them, and the *right culture* to allow risk and experimentation to take hold. It is about catalyzing innovative thinking and having the right context to turn that thinking into action. Innovation is not inherent within organizations—it is developed and nurtured. Unique to nonprofit innovation is a recognition that competing priorities, lack of incentives for innovation, resource constraints, and social problems of immense proportions mean that nonprofit organizations need to work harder to purposefully build solutions that are integrated into the existing fabric of the organization. Thankfully, hard work is nothing new for nonprofits.

Before diving into your first innovation project, there are a few preparatory steps to take in order to initiate dialogue and instill a culture of innovation within your organization. In Chapter 3, we outlined literature and practice wisdom that supports an environment that is ready for social innovation. In Part II, we provide the steps to get you there. This means exposing staff to innovation concepts and activities to capture their interest in learning, embracing, and doing more with innovation. This chapter, *Initiate*, provides concrete actions to prepare you and your organization to establish innovation as a core principle and energize staff to innovate from within.

THE TEAMWORK APPROACH TO INNOVATION

Although there are endless pathways to innovation, we focus on one that sees *innovation teams* as a core principle, and we do this for several reasons. For starters, this is a pivotal way of escaping the "individual genius" mentality. Far too often, we wait for an individual genius to come up with a groundbreaking idea. This requires time, patience—and not to mention the genius, which may not come around (or stay) too frequently. Instead, a team approach allows us to purposefully and mindfully build the right environment for innovation to emerge. Teams build on the ideas of others and share insights, concerns, and questions to come up with promising ideas. These ideas tend to generate greater buy-in because they are seen as being representative of a greater group of people and not a top-down approach.

Innovation shouldn't be a lonely endeavor. Instead, it should be a lively, high-spirited process which fosters idea-sharing from multiple stakeholders. Teams provide a rare space for contrasting ideas and perspectives to merge and flourish. When the relationship-building in the team is effective, team members are enthusiastic about being a part of the group and sharing in its mission. This collaborative energy is instrumental for innovation.

Beginning something new is always labor intensive regardless of its scope. Teams also allow for tasks and priorities to be shared, making the innovation process and successful implementation more easily possible. When your innovation team is well-established, your organization will be set up to ideate and integrate innovation projects of various sizes. Teamwork will be the driving force in guiding your efforts and launching your innovations not just once, but time and again. Once teams have established their innovation mindset, developed team cohesion, and become comfortable with the innovation process, they will be well-poised for launching innovations repeatedly.

Teams are a critical part to building the context for innovation. But creating an intentional context to support innovation is also about culture. It is about galvanizing the staff and leadership to embrace innovation. *Initiate* will help you develop the right context, energize those around you, and build the team that will embolden innovation.

CREATE THE CULTURE FOR INNOVATION

You know about innovation and the potential for nonprofit organizations to contribute substantially. You're excited about the potential impact it will have in solving the social problems that you care about. But what does an innovative nonprofit actually look like? What are the key characteristics that support innovation? Innovation in nonprofit organizations is related to several organizational characteristics including size, flexible funding, board characteristics, and diversity. But beyond these large organizational characteristics, nonprofits can deliberately create a culture that supports innovation. In Chapter 3 we talked about the characteristics of an organization that is ready for innovation; in this section, we talk about how to build that culture.

*IN*fluence staff receptivity to innovation by allocating time, compensation, and other resources for innovation.

*IN*terject bits of innovation exercises into what you are already doing to begin to embed innovation skill sets into your work culture.

*IN*stitutionalize opportunities for innovation.

*IN*vigorate participation from diverse stakeholders from the executive director to the populations you work with.

An innovative nonprofit can take on many different forms, but the ones who establish themselves as forward-thinking agencies integrate the following key characteristics into their organizational culture. Actively integrating these building blocks for innovation is a primer for making innovation part of your organization's DNA. The strategies outlined will support your ability to foster a culture of innovation within your organization:

- Learn to tolerate risk (and celebrate mistakes)
- Foster diverse collaborations and relationships
- Establish rituals to embolden innovation
- Create the space for innovation
- Institute flexible clocks
- Determine clear metrics for accountability

LEARN TO TOLERATE RISK (AND CELEBRATE MISTAKES)

If you look back far enough, all the "best practices" that we now know and incorporate into our services were once experimental, groundbreaking ideas. While we think it important to integrate mainly what has been proved to work into our nonprofit—and rightfully so—it is equally important to think outside the box and try out new initiatives with a bit of chance involved. This does not mean to try just "any old thing," but it does mean being open to new, possibly outlandish ideas and being curious enough to explore their potential. Taking this one step further, innovative organizations are willing to invest resources in a bit of experimentation with these new ideas, knowing full well that while they may be promising, the success of these innovations is uncertain—we call this taking calculated risks.

To get to the stage where you can take a calculated risk, innovative organizations are purposeful about creating opportunities for experimentation. This can be anything from holding sporadic ideation sessions to organizing hackathons, to hosting an innovation retreat, to allocating specific time for innovation processes. Not only does this say the organization supports new ideas, but it takes it a step further by saying the organization also puts in place critical mechanisms to help staff and stakeholders generate new ideas. Nonprofits have a strong track record of coming up with new ideas. What becomes more challenging, however, is when we begin to talk about investing resources into prototyping and testing them.

Nonprofits have scarce resources, and if they're not being utilized to the best of an organization's capacity, it can be alarming for administrators and funders. This is why it's important to instill a culture of innovation and reframe the agency's mindset about the value of testing new ideas in a cost-effective manner through prototyping. Making mistakes is an unavoidable and necessary part of the innovation process! We can learn a lot from experimentation, even when initiatives don't go as planned. When we take a critical (but nonjudgmental) look at what happened, we can see areas for improvement and grow from these experiences. This also reduces the amount of time and energy many people expend trying to sweep a mistake under the rug, allowing us to redirect those resources into learning from the mistake instead of hiding from it.

Mistake-Away Activity

1. Prior to the activity, have everyone submit one recent risk they took that did not yield the expected result.
2. Select one or two to use as case studies.
3. Gather to share the stories and discuss:
   a. What happened?
   b. What went well? What didn't go so well?
   c. What are multiple ways of viewing problem?
   d. Discuss if anyone else has been in this position.
   e. Explore three possible actions to take and their respective consequences.
   f. What are the takeaways from these risks? Ask how can you can learn from them and apply this to the broader agency context?
4. Create a "Mistake-Away Wall" that showcases the risks people have taken for the sake of furthering your agency's mission. Every time you get together to share mistakes, add it to the wall to highlight the bravery and learning that took place.

The mistake-away activity allows you to create learning opportunities from mistakes and allows you to acknowledge that not only do you encourage people to try new things, but that it's also okay to make mistakes along the way! Having mistakes out in the open will allow for more energy spent learning from them and less energy spent trying to cover them up.

There are many ways that mistakes can be utilized as a constructive stage for discussion. If a new online platform failed to attract the audience the organization expected, important questions can be assessed such as, "What were the marketing opportunities we didn't utilize?" "What could improve accessibility?" "How could the design be made more user-friendly?" Innovative nonprofits ask these questions, and they ask them regularly. Rather than fearing failure, they celebrate their ability to acknowledge setbacks and learn from that experience. This prepares them to be more informed the next time they set out to launch new ideas.

FOSTER DIVERSE COLLABORATIONS
AND RELATIONSHIPS

Organizations flourish in the presence of diversity. The bigger the range of backgrounds and experiences among staff members, the richer the conversations and perspectives shared. Developing diverse collaborations involves connecting representatives from a wide array of unlikely suspects coming together to address a shared goal. This means nurturing diversity in the organization as a whole as well as within specific projects. Innovative nonprofits create multiple opportunities for cross-collaboration. These collaborations should integrate players whose backgrounds span the spectrum in terms of age, gender, ethnicity, ability, position within the organization (management, support, and direct service), and relationship with the organization (beneficiary, funder, board member, etc.).

Moreover, it is not enough to be merely open to diversity; we must express this explicitly as a core value of the organization. Doing so reinforces that people of all backgrounds should not only feel welcomed into the agency, but are, in fact, intentionally sought after and invited. Their rich perspectives and experiences broaden and deepen the overall understanding of the issues addressed by nonprofits. Diverse perspectives yield broad problem definition and refinement. They lead to the widest array of solutions and may take the organization on new paths. Being explicit about the importance and value of diversity will demonstrate to others a true commitment to an inclusive, nonhierarchical approach, which is key for innovation.

In medium and large nonprofits, rarely do employees have the opportunity to engage in work with people from other departments. Bringing together unlikely subjects also means including people from all across the organization. When staff members are allowed to establish relationships across various ranks and departments, you enhance cohesion and collaboration within the agency. Communication becomes easier when you know someone in another department and are able to build trust through teamwork. Moreover, a diverse innovation team will be able to challenge each other's assumptions and biases because of the distinctive lens through which they see the organization. A funder will see an issue in a different light than a direct service staff member. A program coordinator will see an issue differently from an HR professional. Thinking through issues from multiple perspectives helps strengthen the likelihood of a solution being well-informed and relevant. Engaging a wide set of participants in innovation helps ensure broad support for testing and implementation.

ESTABLISH RITUALS TO EMBOLDEN INNOVATION

Commitment to innovation means establishing a cultural mindset within the organization that recognizes innovation as a key value. Nurturing such an atmosphere requires time and persistence. Emboldening innovation means taking a dynamic approach to being an organization that is committed to infusing innovation into the work systems and processes. It means valuing ideas and contributions from all stakeholders. It means having a work culture that naturally supports and motivates entrepreneurial thinking. Emboldening innovation means that staff members are inspired to explore, wonder, ideate, and share their ideas in hopes to grow organizational impact.

Examples from the Field

Playworks

Playworks offers a staff recess of 15 minutes to engage in play-based activity. By stopping and playing, staff get to live the mission of the organization and open their mind to creativity.

Other rituals including staff high-fives at the end of meetings and senior management meetings called "The Huddle" to support the passion they are driving to develop at the organization. Small but meaningful rituals help employees feel connected and inspired by the organization's mission.

A creative workforce doesn't happen overnight. Rather, mechanisms put into place over time help generate a culture of innovation: a stimulating work environment; workplace competitions; recognition of promising ideas; time, space, and materials for creativity; incentives for developing and implementing innovative ideas. Organizations like Playworks share rituals that support innovation and creativity (Commongood Careers 2016).

Workplaces that value innovation find multiple ways to incentivize employees and discover new ways of inspiring innovation. While some people are effortlessly creative, others benefit from the additional support of activities and programs. Many more people will engage in creative processes if given the time, resources, and incentive to make it happen. People are more apt to participate if it becomes part of the work rather than an add-on to the work. *Practice makes progress*, and the more practice people have with creativity and experimentation, the more natural it will feel to think outside the box. Moreover, when staff understands this as a core value of the agency, they will feel safe sharing new ideas, knowing that this kind of thinking is highly regarded by the organization.

When innovation happens within organizations, it's rarely a solitary pursuit. Teamwork and cooperation play big roles in the development and execution of innovative programs. By establishing rituals for innovation, an organization is also setting the foundation for teamwork and cross-agency collaboration. Rituals for innovation create a unifying thread among staff members, one that fosters cohesion throughout the organization.

Through these rituals, staff members at various levels of the organization become more comfortable with elements critical for innovation such as ideation, experimentation, and collaboration. Establishing this framework helps shed fears around innovation and allows an organization to transform itself from one that says "But, we've always done it that way" to one that says "Let's give it a try."

CREATE THE SPACE FOR INNOVATION

Rituals and processes support innovation, but physical space also says a lot about what is accepted and expected. Provide the message that "innovation lives here." Organizations that purposefully design their space for innovation consistently reinforce creativity, experimentation, and collaboration. Physical spaces can include collaborative work space; use of natural, raw, or unexpected materials; varied lighting sources; and varied architectural or design features (e.g., varied color choices, welcoming or non–office style furniture, and individualized designs).

Spaces that encourage collaboration, socialization, and flexibility encourage new thinking. Open spaces for networking or spontaneous interaction encourage new thinking. Furniture that is mobile signals flexibility and empowerment. Even small, simple enhancements of physical space can spark encouragement and creativity through art, slogans, quotes, or photographs. Examples of success or innovation in the nonprofit sector might stimulate inspiration and new thinking.

Materials within the space matter, too. Innovation spaces have materials for creation—things like clay, wood, glue, fabric, paint, and art supplies indicate that different ways of imagining are tolerated. The availability of technology indicates its centrality to the work. White boards, markers, and Post-it notes suggest that ideas are not fixed. Iteration is expected. Creativity is celebrated. This environment not only allows innovation, but fosters and encourages it.

INSTITUTE FLEXIBLE CLOCKS

Creating a purposeful time for innovation not only shows commitment to new ideas, but it also demonstrates an organization's commitment to its employee's development and workplace advancement. Organizations that have flexible clocks know that it is important for staff members to be able to step away from their current projects to work on innovation because they see the big picture value of improving organizational culture, creating a workplace balance, enhancing employee cohesion, and using innovation initiatives to produce long-term impact.

Although it's true that staff members are often already working full steam ahead on established projects, allowing flexible time to engage in a different project can be a breath of fresh air. Sometimes the benefit lies in the ability to switch gears and reenergize on a different task; other times it's the creative and animated nature of innovation projects that resonates with staff members. A break from the routine tends to create a happier work balance—as long as the project is one that staff members are committed to and are genuinely enthusiastic about. The more time and energy personally invested in the innovation project, the more committed an employee is to the success and development of that idea.

Examples from the Field

Equal Exchange

Ten percent of employee time can be used as flex formation for independent employee education and/or to advance the mission of the organization. During this time, employees have the option of participating in a relaxed 1-hour educational seminar arranged by the organization.

Once approved by a manager, 10% time can also be used for

- Trainings
- Language classes
- Coalition-building with similar nonprofits
- Participating in a race with a team from the agency
- Self-care
- Sitting on the board of an organization
- Translation of agency materials
- Mentoring

DETERMINE CLEAR METRICS FOR ACCOUNTABILITY

When developing social innovations, we must act with the certainty that the work being done results in positive social impact. By their very nature, innovations involve greater risk and less predictability and thereby hamper clear definitions of success and accountability. Innovation metrics help orient organizations toward the desired future by setting specific goals, putting regular checkpoints in place, recognizing small wins along the way, and keeping a focus on the outcomes of programs. In social innovation, social impact is our true north and we must establish clear indicators that can inform us that what we are doing indeed has the impact intended.

While checkpoints provide an opportunity for correction, they also provide an opportunity to "think small." Innovation is about small wins. Small wins mean celebrating success in parts. Acknowledging success at regular intervals rather than waiting for the conclusion of specific projects allows good ideas to flourish and gain more momentum. Small wins may relate to a specific project or may relate to organizational changes, staff, or process. They may relate to overall innovation projects, but celebrating small wins helps you stay on track until the big wins occur.

Agencies serious about large-scale change need to examine their efforts against social impact metrics. While evaluating the success of our programs is a key element of nonprofit organizational work, it is especially important to get this right in innovation, where we run the risk of having limited impact—or worse, possibly having a negative impact on the communities we work with. As nonprofits, we must be accountable to our stakeholders and to our mission, which means that when we develop new programs, we need a clear understanding of the direction in which we want to go and the impact we want to see, and we must have evaluation systems for getting us there. At the core of every monitoring and evaluation system are clear goals and objectives. Peter Drucker's SMART (specific, measurable, assignable, relevant, time-bound) criteria for objectives will help establish a solid foundation for any new initiative and provides an important starting point for tracking success (Drucker 1954). When we clearly define the objectives of an innovation, it becomes easier to associate it with indicators of success and a monitoring system to ensure these goals are met. Since innovation is experimental, we must always be checking in with our established indicators to measure how well we are reaching our objectives and if any course correction might be needed.

Organizations involved in innovation must be committed to ongoing evaluation. Multiple avenues exist for evaluating new social initiatives. Among the most useful are *formative evaluations*, which look at the way in which a process is being applied, and *summative evaluations*, which look at the outcomes of social programs. Both are essential, and both must be put into place and carefully tracked. Are our initiatives being implemented the way we envisioned? Are we reaching our target population? Are our programs following the ethical standards of the nonprofit? How are programs being received? Is our theory of change validated in our outcomes? Do participants feel empowered through participation in our programs? All of these questions and more are needed to take an honest look at what's being done and make any necessary corrections.

Not all innovations are successful, and that's okay. What is not okay is leaving evaluation to the side and disregarding when the innovation is ineffective. By doing so, not only do we poorly invest our limited resources, but we also risk causing harm to the community. Take the 1994 Violent Crime Control Act implemented by Bill Clinton, for example. When it was implemented, the bill was seen as a breakthrough paradigm shift innovation that would keep repeat offenders off the streets by significantly increasing the prison sentences of persons convicted of a felony after their third offense. While applauded by many at the time, the long-term unintended consequences of the bill have resulted in a 171% explosion of the prison system with a vastly disproportionate impact on black Americans (Alexander 2011). This is exactly the kind of impact which we must be concerned about. The success of an innovation is not always clear in the beginning. Monitoring and evaluation must be in place to ensure we are seeing positive impact where intended and making corrections anywhere else.

In the context of *innovation from within*, assessing success also means checking in periodically to ensure that new initiatives are aligned with the organization's existing programs and consistent with the agency's mission. Creating synchronicity between an innovation and the nonprofit's work will help ensure that programs are complementary and support each other's success.

MOBILIZE INNOVATORS WITHIN YOUR ORGANIZATION

Because innovation flourishes in the right culture, we must be strategic in how we develop and nurture our nonprofit culture. An important task of an intrapreneur is to cultivate that culture within our organizations. Little by little, there are strategies that intrapreneurs can integrate into the workplace to initiate an organizational culture that reflects the characteristics of an innovative organization as previously described.

Working within traditional structures may be challenging. Many times, people will be adverse to change and will feel apprehensive about new ideas. A progressive integration of new organizational norms will help staff better adapt and embrace innovation principles—but remember, this won't happen overnight. There are some strategic actions, however, that intrapreneurs can take to mobilize innovators within the agency and initiate a culture of innovation.

PLAY WITH A PURPOSE: TIME AND SPACE FOR INNOVATION

One key way to establish a mindset and capacity for innovation among staff is to provide hands-on activities to learn about innovation and practice the skills involved. To some, the idea of innovation is alluring. To others, innovation sounds like something better left to engineers and programmers. Purposefully cultivating innovators is about creating opportunities and space for creativity to emerge.

A first step to making innovation exciting is to make it accessible. Offer opportunities for people to learn about innovation and what it means in the context of nonprofits. Provide practice sessions where employees engage in innovation activities and get to "try-on" this start-up mentality. Educate others by providing examples of other nonprofits doing innovative work. This provides everyone with a baseline understanding of what innovation can look like within the nonprofit sector. Bring people together to practice skills like ideation, rapid prototyping, or open innovation. The more the environment is open to and interested in innovation, the more activities that can be incorporated. With mindful and persistent infusion of innovation practices, innovation will embed itself into the organizational culture.

Innovation capacity can take several forms at the organization. A first level of engagement might begin with occasional social innovation talks, workshops, or trainings. These efforts can begin to generate modest interest in innovation and can open the door for more in the future. Bite-size innovation experiences might stimulate new discussions or catalyze new relationships. By integrating practical exercises like the Root Cause Activity, you can spark lively discussions about the social issues your organization addresses while developing foundational innovation skill sets.

Root Cause Activity

1. As a group, discuss root causes and why it is important to iden-tify and address issues at the base of the problem, rather than (or in addition to) the more visible consequences of those problems.
2. Distribute the root cause worksheet (see Figure 4.2). As a group, go through a couple of examples (i.e., high teen pregnancy rates or increase in no-shows) to understand how root cause works and its learning opportunities.
3. Collectively identify a problem the agency is looking at. After coming to a decision, have people work through the root cause worksheet in pairs.
4. Discuss findings as a group.

The Root Cause Activity is a tool that helps you uncover the deep-seated causes of a social problem by having you to look deeper and question the underlying issues. Social innovation aims to identify and address the causes of social injustices rather than the consequences, thereby investing our resources where they can generate greater impact. A Root Cause Analysis can be instrumental in identifying areas within your nonprofit that require action.

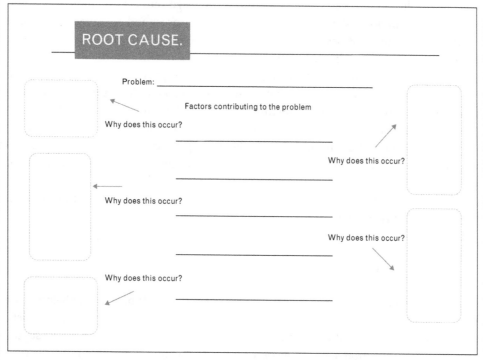

FIGURE 4.2: Root cause analysis.

Nonprofits that take the next level of commitment to innovation may establish programs within their organizations, such as innovation suggestion boxes, or develop formal innovation teams. Putting a spin on the traditional suggestion box, innovation suggestion boxes recognize the valuable expertise of employees at all levels of the organization. They encourage employees to submit proposals for programs or strategies that can be implemented by the organization to respond to a need they've seen in the community. The ideas submitted in the suggestion box are reviewed by the organizational leadership, including the board. If the proposal shows promise and is worth implementing, the employee is recognized formally and is given an award for his or her creativity and proactivity.

As organizations progress in their innovation capacity, new opportunities to stimulate innovation are needed. If the staff is eager to engage in more innovation, the organization might consider integrating innovation challenges. These challenges might include suggestions to make the office more environmentally sustainable or find creative uses for discarded items around the office. Winners from these challenges may be recognized for their efforts by offering prizes or recognizing an "Innovation Genius" within your agency. If the organization has the capacity, you might consider specific "start-up weekends" or "hackathon" style events that allow staff to fully immerse in solution development.

If the organization is ready, more elaborate structures to support innovation might become possible, including ongoing innovation labs, the development of innovation departments, or dedicated innovation staff. The development of an innovation department can be a major driver in promoting an innovative organizational culture. The department can decide to provide a multitude of innovation opportunities. Some innovation departments might decide to coordinate competitions or design retreats for employees. Others may decide to develop a structured social innovation process and encourage the creation of ideas from within. Systems like these motivate employees to think outside the box and reinforce the value of their contributions.

Establishing innovation as a core value means moving your organization beyond simply offering one-time projects or activities. It means regularly incorporating innovation throughout the organization and embodying a culture that promotes creativity. It means having the leadership of the organization on board as champions of social innovation. It means dedicating necessary resources to teaching and practicing innovation. It means that the organization understands that when everyone at the agency is involved in and committed to innovation, it increases the likelihood of developing successful new programs. An organization oriented toward innovation will invest in the development and sustainability of new ideas because it's part of its DNA.

LEAD THE LEADERS

Staff buy-in from all levels of the organization is critical, but it is particularly helpful when the executive leadership of the organization is committed to innovation. Having administrators at this level on board with innovation can be a major driving force in generating support and mobilizing innovation. Depending on your position within the agency, it may be easier or more difficult to get these players on board. One of the most frequent downfalls of new initiatives is the lack of support from leadership. Far too often we see innovative projects with great potential fail because the leadership of the agency does not see it as a priority or does not feel invested in the initiative—generate buy-in from the start to give innovation the best chance to flourish.

If executive leadership drives innovation from the beginning, getting lower level staff to be interested and engaged becomes more critical. On the flip side, if the people driving the innovation are staff members with less authority, meetings with top leadership are an imperative. During these conversations, discuss the ways in which innovation helps enhance the organization's mission. Making clear connections between innovation practices and the ways in which they will enhance the overall mission will create greater buy-in for innovation. In general, evaluating for mission fit should be a regular benchmark during your innovation practice to ensure that your projects are aligned with your mission.

It might also be helpful to use promising innovation examples from within your field when talking to organizational leaders about the potential for integrating innovation. Exploring the rich possibilities that innovation can create and looking at what is already being done can be inspiring. It can also make the impact of innovation in your field more tangible to those with limited exposure to innovation.

Facts and figures can be powerful and influential to this audience. Another compelling strategy is to describe the potential impact of innovation through storytelling. Although oral and written storytelling has a long history, radio, graphic novels, podcasts, and videos have far expanded the boundaries of storytelling. Through narratives, we can appeal to the emotional and practical sides of those we are trying to reach. Inspire the leadership of your organization to share your enthusiasm for innovation by sharing an inspirational story that conveys the potential of innovation and its impact.

Storytelling Activity

1. Find your inspiration. Your inspiration can come from a personal experience or from an outside source you have learned about. Think about the message you want to convey and the audience for whom it's intended.
2. Choose your medium. Traditional spoken storytelling is great. You also have other options to consider: poetry, spoken word, PowerPoint, radio, podcast, infographic, visual art, and more. Again, be sure to consider your audience!
3. Develop your story. Include the following elements in your story: the hook, the inspiration, the turning point, the call to action. Make clear the connection between the story and its relevance to your organization.
4. Share it. Your story can be shared on multiple platforms. Consider whether it is something that you would like to share with others. Storytelling has far-reaching potential.

Additional tips:

- Include arguments to appeal to hearts and minds
- Be authentic
- Make the call to action clear and compelling

More and more, we are honing in on our ability to break down barriers through the power of stories. They help us share intimate moments in compelling ways. When meeting with people who might be skeptical about the potential of innovation, storytelling can help provide a different perspective and imagine new possibilities. This activity can also come in handy throughout other parts of your innovation process.

In addition to scheduling meetings to explore how innovation can benefit the organization, consider conducting a formal innovation audit of the organization to assess strengths and room for improvement. Looking at the agency's commitment, ability, and readiness for innovation can spur concrete areas for organizational growth and will be a useful tool for piquing the interest of the executive leadership.

Innovation Audit Activity

1. Distribute the questions in Handout 4.1 to members of your organization and allow them some time to rank the organization on each question on a scale of 1–5, with 1 being strongly disagree and 5 being strongly agree.

HANDOUT 4.1: Innovation Audit

As an organization we . . .

1. Allocate financial resources to innovation.

   1   2   3   4   5

2. Offer trainings on innovation topics such as rapid prototyping, user-centered design, creativity, and innovative research strategies.

   1   2   3   4   5

3. Establish processes, rituals, and reward systems for innovation.

   1   2   3   4   5

4. Embrace risk-taking as a necessary part of innovation.

   1   2   3   4   5

5. Engage in discussions about understanding root cause and reframing issues and problems.

    1   2   3   4   5

6. Utilize technological resources as key resources in enhancing social impact.

    1   2   3   4   5

7. Invite unlikely suspects in the co-development, co-implementation, and evaluation of new initiatives.

    1   2   3   4   5

8. Evaluate the progress and impact of initiatives.

    1   2   3   4   5

9. Tap into nontraditional funding streams such as crowdfunding, social enterprise models, venture capitalist funding, or social impact investing.

    1   2   3   4   5

10. Regularly scan the environment for potential partners from diverse sectors.

    1   2   3   4   5

Total:

2. Have each person total their audits and calculate the averages of each question and for the innovation audit as a whole.
3. Use the averages to analyze how well your organization practices innovation. On an overall level, how well does your organization embrace innovation? What is your organization doing well, and where must you grow? Discuss your results as a group.

The innovation audit can help you identify how firmly your organization embraces innovation. What contributes to the success of the high-scoring activities? Which areas need the most attention? What can be done to address them? Whose support is needed? This information is useful as a base for discussion among staff at various levels within the organization. A high-scoring innovation audit will give you confidence to continue in the innovation process, knowing you have broad organizational support embedded within the organization. The results of the innovation audit can and should be used to discuss overall organizational goals. The audit can be applied on an annual basis to benchmark your organization's progress. Keep a record of the scores because they can be helpful to compare the organization's trajectory of innovation.

There are many different ways to get general staff engaged in innovation. You might want to begin by considering some of the reasons and motivators that first captured your own interest in innovation. Take the time to consider these reasons and think about how some of those can be used to inspire others into taking action. In addition to those, convey the professional reasons why others should want to get on board with innovation. You might share some of the following reasons: the chance to get out of your comfort zone and have fun, the opportunity to engage leadership within the agency, the potential to be part of a team-based collaboration, the development of skills such as design thinking and rapid prototyping, or the possibility of seeing your ideas turn into programs, products, and services with real impact. Find out what motivates others and build on that ambition.

While it's not realistic to get every single staff member interested and actively involved in innovation, there are actions you can take to still include everyone in the dialogue. For example, if you conduct an innovation audit, invite others to contribute their opinions or suggestions. If the leadership of the organization is on board with the idea, consider making the findings available to the staff. Make your work an open and transparent process by sharing results with people across the organization. The greater the engagement in innovation practice and dialogue, the better.

Beyond just informing the staff of any innovative initiatives being implemented, let people know *why* innovation is taking on a more significant role within the organization. Remember that people have had mixed experiences with new ideas and initiatives—making concepts like innovation and change particularly unsettling to some people. Greater involvement and transparency will help assuage some of these biases and concerns.

After reaching out to both leadership and staff, it's a good idea to take a step back and get a meta-perspective of the level of commitment to innovation.

- What does your organizational landscape of innovation look like?
- Does the board see innovation in the same way as the executive director? How about the direct service staff? Mid-level management?
- What do outside stakeholders have to say?
- Who are your greatest allies in promoting innovation? Can they be leveraged in addressing any resistance that you may have encountered?
- Who or what presents barriers or obstacles to moving innovation forward? Can these be changed? Can innovation still move forward despite these challenges?
- What kinds of communication strategies can reinforce a cultural shift toward innovation?

Informally assess these questions and set goals for any that may be relevant to your nonprofit's context. Keep these considerations in mind as you move forward with building your innovation team and make sure to revisit them to gauge the level of progress and any additional measures that should be taken to address outstanding concerns.

BUILD YOUR INNOVATION TEAM

While innovation can take place using many different formats, our work and previous work in innovation suggest the power of the innovation team. Building an effective innovation team is a consequential step of the process. Your innovation team will be the engine that will generate ideas and turn them into reality. This core team will be responsible for going through the stages of the innovation process: *Initiate, Investigate, Innovate,* and *Integrate.* Having the right people on board will significantly impact the team's ability to fulfill its goals successfully. The team might be established for this one project or play a longer, more formal role in an ongoing way. While teams can be formed in infinite combinations, building the *right* team is critical.

Typically, new initiatives and programs are created by the executive leadership of the organization. In social innovation, however, ideas are sparked through a collaborative process that purposefully integrates unlikely suspects. In addition to the traditional leadership, these innovation teams are comprised of stakeholders from in and around the organization. This sometimes means direct service employees and administrative staff working collaboratively alongside program beneficiaries and management-level employees. The confluence of personal experience and organizational influence has innumerable layers of benefits.

Teams made of diverse stakeholders have the broadest understanding of the problem and therefore present the widest range of solutions. Diverse teams allow sharing across different perspectives and different relationships with the issue. Contrary to the programs traditionally created by the executive leadership of an agency, programs generated through a participatory innovation process tend to gain more support because they have strong input and buy-in from stakeholders at multiple levels. In addition to being a program that reflects the views of different constituents, team members then become ambassadors for the program, sharing with other people in their circles about their experiences and the efforts that went into the development of the program. Because established nonprofits are often faced with the challenge of resistance to new programs, this momentum is very helpful in generating enthusiasm and support for new innovations from within.

INVITE THE RIGHT PEOPLE

To set your team up for success, you must reach out to the right people. A strong innovation team can make the difference between one which struggles to adopt new approaches and one which embraces the challenge of attempting new strategies. To actively draw the right people in, reach out to them individually. Personal invitations can go a long way. Invite those who have demonstrated an interest in innovation or offer a unique skill set that may benefit the innovation team. Tell them why you think *they specifically* would be a good addition to the team and what skills and attributes they possess that you value. It is important for people to know that you're not looking for just any social innovation team, you're looking for the *right* social innovation team.

Build on the innovation dialogue that you have been initiating within your organization. What has worked in getting people's interest? What can you expand on? Who are your allies in promoting innovation? Utilize this enthusiasm to encourage others to join. Having team members who are excited and dedicated to innovation will greatly improve the experience and outcome.

Depending on the size of your agency, your innovation team will vary in size. Ideally, the size of your team is somewhere between 6 and 12 people. This is large enough to include an array of people and perspectives, but small enough so that everyone's voice is heard. The following guidelines will provide considerations for building your innovation team with the right innovators.

ENTHUSIASM

Who is the most excited about innovation at the agency? It shouldn't be about convincing people to join the team. It should be about leveraging existing enthusiasm to energize collaboration and innovation. Where is there curiosity and desire for personal and organizational growth? Build on the spark within people who want to catalyze change.

INFLUENCE

Ensure that staff with varying levels of influence are integrated into the team. Having various positions within the organization represented will be helpful at different stages of the innovation process. Direct-level employees have regular interactions with the organization's stakeholders and social issues. Administrative staff have insight on facilitating work flow and working in teams that improves communication and cooperation. Board members provide a meta-perspective and strategic view. Executive leadership will provide critical support during implementation and decision-making. In addition to their unique perspectives, all will become ambassadors and help promote buy-in for your innovation.

DIVERSITY

The more perspectives included, the stronger the results of the team. Greater diversity among the team will mean that your process and resulting innovation will be informed by various points of view. For example, having gender balance in the innovation team means it is likely to be in tune with nuanced issues pertaining to gender bias. An intergenerational innovation team will mean greater consideration for how people of different ages might interact with your innovation. Program beneficiaries or allies are a great addition to your team; they add outside perspective and have a lived experience that is critical. It brings their views front and center and helps the team develop solutions that will be accepted by the community.

TABLE 4.1: Traits of successful innovation teams	
As individuals:	As a team:
Committed	Diverse
Curious	Organized
Flexible	Fun and enthusiastic
Good listeners	Open communication
Active contributors of opinions and critiques	Prideful
Team players	Well-connected

COMMITMENT

Although level of commitment can vary depending on what the team decides, the investment each person makes will be significant, and a person's ability to commit should be taken into account when building the team. Team members should be flexible sharing and balancing innovation responsibilities with other work. They should be willing to go the extra mile at times to make it work. Be sure to clarify with administration the time and dedication that the innovation process will take so that team members feel comfortable allocating the necessary time and resources to the innovation process.

Teams will take on various shapes and forms. Table 4.1 lists those characteristics that represent traits of successful innovation teams.

SET THE GROUNDWORK FOR SUCCESS

Once your team members have been identified, it's time to get together to begin your innovation process and think through some practical considerations. These first few gatherings are likely to set the tone for future meetings, so place special attention on the environment and energy. Get together in a casual setting. Is there a space for informal meetings at your organization? Is gathering at a local coffee shop an option? How about the park down the street? The setting will inspire the flow of the meeting, so be mindful about your selection.

Depending on the nature and size of the organization, some teams will already know each other well, while other teams are meeting people from their organization for the first time. Even if team members already have a relationship with each other, start off with an activity to get to know each other on a more personal level—the more you can facilitate meaningful interaction, the stronger the team dynamics and the more fruitful the innovation process becomes.

Identify the overall goals and expectations of the innovation team so everyone is on the same page from the get-go. The Envision Innovation Activity can help team members get a sense for the hopes and dreams each person has for the organization. Have it be a participatory process so the ideas evolve in an organic manner rather than seeming imposed. Utilize the considerations in the next section to start your team off on the right foot and think through some of the critical elements for success.

Envision Innovation Activity

1. Give everyone a blank piece of paper and ask everyone to divide the page into three sections (top, middle, bottom).
2. Have each person use the top section to draw what they hope the organization will be like in the future. In the bottom section, have them draw the current state of the organization. In the middle section, have people envision what needs to happen to transform the organization from the bottom representation to the top picture.
3. Go around the group and have people describe the transition they would like to see in the organization and/or community. Use this activity as a platform for discussing how innovation can be used to get the agency to transform your organization to its ideal state.

A simple visioning exercise can be an effective tool to spark conversation and curiosity. You can use this as part of an innovation seminar or even as part of a quick icebreaker before a staff meeting. This activity can be adapted to fit any context in which you want people to imagine a different future and think of actions that will make that reality possible. This can be reutilized during other phases of the innovation process.

BOOST TEAM DYNAMICS

EXPLORE INDIVIDUAL AND TEAM HOPES

Discover each other's motivations for both becoming part of the team and for working in their distinct part of the organization. It's not often that we get the opportunity to discuss our motivations for doing this kind of work. Also worth discussing are the strengths each person brings to the table. People are full of hidden talent. These conversations can be very influential in developing strong rapport with each other and for inspiring the team to dream big.

BEGIN A PROJECT TIMELINE

A typical innovation process will span a minimum of 4 months from the initiation of the team's efforts through the integration of the solution. Depending on several factors (including topic chosen, availability of team members, simultaneous projects, and period of beta testing), this will vary by team and organization.

DETERMINE TIME AND SPACE FOR MEETINGS

Discuss where the team like would to meet on an ongoing basis. A space that isn't your typical meeting area would be ideal, but convenience and access to other spaces are certainly considerations for the team to keep in mind. If the team has to meet in a traditional space, consider mixing it up every once in awhile to keep things interesting. What times and frequency work best for the team? This will be a good discussion to reinforce the fundamental principles of cooperation and flexibility.

ESTABLISH ACCOUNTABILITY

How will you check in with each other? Weekly emails? Video calls on an as-needed basis? Face-to-face meetings every other week? What will you do to hold each other accountable to agreed upon tasks? Who will handle this process? Having clear expectations for oneself and each other will help the team start off on the right foot.

DISCUSS COMMUNICATION

In addition to communication within the team, how will you reach out to others in the organization? What is the best way to keep staff and leadership involved in what's going on? While you don't want to flood others with information, you do want to keep others in the loop. Ideally, you will also be receiving input from others in the organization to ensure they are connected and heard.

SELECT YOUR TEAM NAME

It may seem like a trivial discussion point, but it's actually constructive to talk about! While being called the "Innovation Team" is certainly okay, the way the team decides to name itself can carry weight. Choose what's right for your team. If you want to take it a step further and create a logo, go for it. The more you can make it your own, the better.

If it would be helpful, plan a final immersion for the team to make sure everyone has a solid understanding of innovation before moving forward. This can be engaging in an innovation 101 seminar, practicing a rapid prototyping activity, hosting a guest speaker, or touring an agency that has an established social innovation lab or project. Document your work along the way. In addition to it being a handy resource, it's a good reminder to pat yourself on the back for your hard work in laying the foundation for innovation!

REFLECTION ON INITIATING FROM WITHIN

1. What does your organization already do that promotes an innovation mindset and what are tangible actions that can be taken tomorrow?
2. How will you know when people in your organization are ready to embrace innovation? What will you notice within the work culture that indicates this openness?
3. What do you envision for the future of the organization and how is it different and/or similar to what others hope for?

MAIN POINTS FOR INITIATING FROM WITHIN

- Innovative organizations don't just offer one-off innovation experiences—they embed innovative practices as part of their DNA. This means fostering many opportunities to engage in innovation and learning from successes and failures.
- A culture of innovation includes being open to risk-taking and celebrating mistakes, fostering diverse collaborations, establishing rituals to embolden innovation, creating a physical space for innovation, instituting flexible clocks to work on additional projects, and having clear evaluation metrics for success.
- Teamwork allows for greater idea sharing, generates greater buy-in for new projects, and creates an upbeat dynamic among those invested in innovation. Ensuring diversity within your organization and innovation team strengthens the impact of your work.
- Generating buy-in is critical for initiating a culture of innovation. Innovation suggestion boxes, hackathons, storytelling, competitions, and innovation workshops are all strategies for engaging the general staff and leadership in innovation and experimentation.
- When building your innovation team, make it a *true* collaborative experience. Bring in people from across the agency and build on their curiosity and enthusiasm for innovation. The opportunity to work with people from all levels of the agency is rare . . . take advantage of that opportunity and express what each person brings to the table.

INVESTIGATE

Chapter 5 provides tools to allow you to identify and analyze a social issue through traditional and innovative methods.

FIGURE 5.1: Investigate model.

Get ready to ...

1. Select the social issue your team will be addressing and express its urgency.
2. Use empathic inquiry to research the issue, understand the context, and identify opportunities.
3. Frame the problem to catalyze broad solution generation.

The most successful social innovations demonstrate a remarkable understanding of their target community, social issue, and available resources. Effective innovations are aware of the multiple dimensions which comprise a given social issue and utilize that insight to design solutions that capture the nuances of the problem. Rather than assuming they know enough about a given problem, strong innovation teams look to critically examine the issue, explore its many facets, and see it in a new light.

Inquiry and analysis are critical competencies for challenging our assumptions of the social issue at hand and learning from the ways in which various stakeholders perceive the problem. Getting to the root cause of the social issue challenges basic assumptions about cause and leads to more robust solutions. A complete understanding of a problem's context allows innovators to identify significant gaps and opportunities surrounding a particular issue. Addressing these gaps is at the heart of social innovation. *This* is where social innovation thrives. *This* is where action must take place.

When we investigate, we take an exploratory approach to social innovation through empathic inquiry (see Figure 5.1). This is what social innovation is about. It is about asking questions, searching for knowledge, and getting deeper into a subject. It is about the humility that comes from asking questions or seeking insight rather than assuming we already have all the information needed to act.

When an organization is ready for social innovation, we need to next identify where we will put our efforts. We begin by setting our sights on areas where our organization can take action. This may be addressing new issues that have come up for our organization, such as services for new populations, or responding to emergent social problems or changes in public policy. It could also mean looking at areas where our organization could strengthen its current endeavors. This could be designing an innovation to breathe new life into a struggling program or updating a program to reflect changes in the cultural context. With new technologies and resources, the possibilities are endless, but, before jumping into action, you first must determine which areas for action are most critical and relevant to your organization and team.

An advantage that we have as nonprofits is an intimate understanding of the populations we work with and the context in which they live. This is an invaluable asset to the innovation process and will serve as a useful launch pad to fully understand the social issue and context your team will identify. In addition to this expertise, your team will delve deeply into the identified problem through various research strategies. By examining the current landscape of your social issue and inquiring with stakeholders, your team will be able to unlock aspects of the problem that were previously hidden. These key areas are important for identifying the root causes of the issue, which will lead to the generation of sustainable solutions.

---

*IN*quire with an empathic approach and be receptive to users as they share their own expertise of the issue.

*IN*voke research studies and field examples to demonstrate to stakeholders the importance of addressing the problem.

*IN*terconnect your research findings to understand relationships between key factors influencing the issue.

Throughout the course of the *Investigate* phase, your understanding of the problem will likely evolve, shift, reshape, and be redefined. The issues at hand are complex and constantly changing. Therefore, our understanding of them must be continually informed and multi-faceted. No doubt, your team brings expertise to this issue, but this phase is an opportunity to broaden that expertise, refine your understanding, and reframe your problem statement. It is an opportunity to look at the problem from multiple perspectives and challenge our assumptions of cause. Deep inquiry provides that space to go deeper and opens the doors to a wide array of opportunities for action. Through the process of investigating the social problem, you and your team will be well-situated to generate solutions that are relevant, well-informed, and in tune with stakeholder views.

DISCOVER YOUR INSPIRATION

Taking action requires interest, commitment, and passion. It is the easy to be excited at the beginning, but finding your team's true inspiration carries them through the challenges and roadblocks in the innovation process. So, while it may seem obvious or it may feel like you already know where you are headed, it is important to take a critical look at your organization and mindfully identify where you and your innovation team want to take action. Several ideas or suggestions will have likely surfaced after the *Initiate* phase at your organization. These topics will serve as a useful platform for beginning to explore an action area with your team.

Opportunities for introspective analysis are rare. Utilize this time to ask important questions, identify areas for improvement within your organization, and discover untapped resources to promote growth. Engage with others whose perspectives are different from your own. In diverse innovation teams, this will come naturally, but, even so, make it a point to connect with stakeholders who have different relationships with the organization. You'll likely find their input informative and refreshing.

FIND PROBLEMS AND OPPORTUNITIES

Even when organizations are on the right track, issues often emerge that could use some attention. Those might consist of issues that have been noted but overshadowed by other organizational needs, or they may truly be emergent problems that your agency has yet to grapple with. If your team knows the issue they would like to address right off the bat, then great: that might be a good place to start your innovation work. But, even if your agency is already running smoothly, there are plenty of other areas where your team can take action. Engaging in innovation doesn't have to mean that your organization is doing something wrong and needs to fix it. It can also mean that you're aware of opportunities for growth and are proactive about embracing promising opportunities. It can mean that you have a vision toward the future and acknowledge that, with a changing context and new resources in technology, what you do and how you do it can be revolutionized. This *Investigate* phase is an opportunity to discover that inspiration.

In your nonprofit, maybe you have seen a change in the population demographics of who you have been serving. Cultural shifts, both on a local and broader level, mean that the context in which we work can change significantly in a relatively short time. Increased immigration from Latin America might mean that your agency has to respond to a cultural and/or language shift in your community. A changing cultural mindset on LGBTQ rights could be a call to action for your organization to specifically target the LGBTQ community. State and federal health care policy changes could alter what is required of your organization, or it could mean a disruption in the services that are available to your stakeholders. In these situations, your organization can utilize innovation practices to adapt its response and commitment to the changing context of your community.

A tried and true method for discovering your inspiration is a simple strengths, weaknesses, opportunities, and threats (SWOT) analysis (Figure 5.2). By stepping back and allowing the team to take an objective look at the organization, areas of priority and/or opportunity begin to surface and can serve as fertile ground for discussion. Take particular note of areas where there may be disagreement or topics where there is a markedly active discussion. These conversation areas are issues that underscore the team's passion—the greater the interest in the topic, the more enthusiasm the team will have in addressing the topic.

While a SWOT analysis is a traditional nonprofit tool that continues to be useful, it can be modified for a more creative approach. The Butterfly Effect Activity is an example of how you can derive the same useful lessons from a SWOT analysis in a more hands-on, interactive manner, making it possible to unearth the same insights and opportunities through creativity and participation.

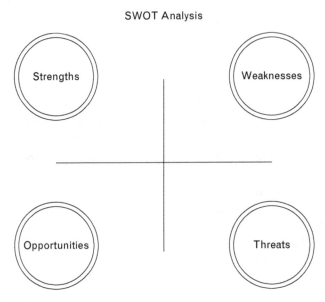

FIGURE 5.2: SWOT analysis.

The Butterfly Effect Activity

1. Ask the team to describe the most relevant trends or factors influencing your organization. Consider the following:
   a. Influences within your organization
   b. Funding streams
   c. Demographic or cultural shifts
   d. Shifts or relationships with other agencies
   e. Policy influences
2. Use dot voting to identify the most important influences identified. The top influences are selected to become "butterflies."
3. Break off into small teams to discuss each butterfly. Using the concept of the butterfly effect (the flap of a single butterfly's wing can have significant ripple effects elsewhere), have each team come up with a story of how the butterfly will grow and develop. How could the organization and its stakeholders be impacted as a result of this butterfly? What will happen in 6 months? 1 year? 5 years?
4. Which of the butterflies' worlds seems to be the most plausible? Which is the most critical? Given the constraints and opportunities present in each butterfly's world, discuss what needs to happen in order for your organization to navigate those possible worlds.

The innovation process can help your agency best prepare for future scenarios. Anticipating the future by examining current trends will help your team identify relevant places to intervene. Take note of how the team reacts to each butterfly world created. Where is there excitement? Disagreement? Promise? Curiosity? Threats? Discuss these topics as potential areas for your team's innovation work.

Another avenue for discovering your inspiration is to consider action through the lens of an idealized future. Building on the same concept as the "Envision Innovation" activity in Chapter 4, imagining what the future can hold for your organization can unlock many potential ideas for action. To kick off conversation with your team, ask them the "Miracle Question" and follow whatever path it might take you. You can ask "Suppose you were to go home today, and while you're away from the office, a miracle happens—and that miracle is that the problems we are now facing have gone away. When you come into the office tomorrow morning, what changes will you notice that will let you know that the miracle has happened?" Team members might say that they have noticed increased engagement from teens, or they might say that they receive phone calls from legislators showing their support. Whatever topics emerge are fair game for integrating into the innovation process.

Don't forget to include input from your agency's target population. Innovation is a collaborative process, and it absolutely should be inclusive of beneficiaries along the way. You can invite them to share ideas through social media, or you can utilize satisfaction surveys to hear directly from the people you serve. The strategies you undertake with your team to discover your inspiration can also be used within the community to unearth priorities from the community's point of view. If you conduct a SWOT analysis with your team, why not with program beneficiaries? The results from your research with the community can be very informative.

The way in which your team diagnoses the problem can be a combination of formal and imaginative approaches. Choose what best fits your team and organization. The goal is to vividly think about what they would like to see in the future and take note of what exactly needs to change in order to make that a reality. What tools and resources are available that tell the team this idealized future is in fact possible. The energy and curiosity that team members have in problem identification will significantly contribute to their passion in generating solutions that are high on impact and innovation.

LOOK AT FIT AND ALIGNMENT

Even after several conversations, selecting where to start may not always be straightforward. In fact, if your team members come from different departments within your organization, they are likely to have different opinions on where your team should take action. Because of this, have the team focus on the one aspect of the organization that is certain to bring them together: the mission. If you have several ideas of where the team should focus, consider ranking the suggestions in terms of how they align with your mission statement. Which priority areas will enhance your organization's commitment to its mission? Which areas will either strengthen areas of work that your organization is currently engaged in or tap into areas of work where your organization *should* be engaged in? In addition to this, integrate your strategic plan into the conversation. In addition to it already outlining upcoming priority areas for the organization, your strategic plan can help your team evaluate how well-aligned the team's vision for the future is with the vision your organization has explicitly detailed.

Funding considerations are an everyday reality for nonprofits. Since at this point in your innovation process the innovation has yet to even be developed, it is difficult to think of how you might get it funded. However, it's still a good idea to look into areas of work that are currently being funded in your field or by your organization's major donors. Consider whether there are resources currently available for funding in the problem areas you want to address. If you already have a strong relationship with a funder, consider linking your innovation work to this cause. Even if it's still too early to apply for funding, having potential funders in mind can open many doors down the road.

The spectrum of opportunities broadens even more when you consider possible collaborations with other agencies. Sometimes teams limit their thinking to the specific resources available internally, but there are likely to be plenty of outside resources that can be leveraged to help you innovate. Think about the various connections that are available to your organization, including your board of directors, previous partnerships, local government leaders, community members, local businesses, and membership organizations. Depending on your project and internal capacity, consider integrating these key stakeholders at various points throughout your innovation process.

Remember that the project you select and the innovation you develop will require buy-in from everyone. The earlier your colleagues are on board with tackling a particular issue, the better. Take the time to talk with people within your agency and get their input. You may choose to go about it in informal terms, like over lunch with coworkers, or you might prefer to schedule a formal meeting with agency leaders to discuss ideas. How you go about it is entirely up to the team and the organization; just make sure you are getting approval for your project at all necessary points along the way.

Use these conversations to get inside people's heads. Do they agree with problem areas that your team has identified? Which ones do they consider to be of highest priority? Did you notice them perk up at the mention of a particular topic? Think of this as beginning to build the momentum for your innovation.

Horserace Activity

1. When you go out to the racetrack, you don't randomly bet on a horse. Instead, you predict which horse has the best bet of winning using different insights. In this activity, each potential problem or opportunity for innovation is a "horse." Begin by brainstorming the top racehorses. Have each team member take ownership of one horse. Of course, like all prize-winning horses, the horse should have a good name, assigned by its owner.
2. Have each owner come up with stats on his or her horse and describe it to the attendees.

   Possible stats:
   - Basic facts: weight, breed, track record (Relevant facts and figures)
   - What is the horse's speed? (How important is it to act fast?)
   - Is this horse a fan favorite? (Does it have stakeholder support?)
   - Is this a distance horse? (Potential for long-term impact)
   - Previous injuries (Any factors that are working against the issue)
   - How well does the horse run on this surface? (Is this good timing to work on this issue?)
3. When all the horses are ready, have them "race" by dot voting.
4. Discuss the top winning horses.

You can certainly have a discussion about which issues are the most critical to act on, but why not make it fun? This activity will help your team identify many facets of the social issues you could possibly address through the innovation process and select which issue you should focus on given your skill set, resources, and context. Use the different horse stats to express a complete picture of the problem. Having the race won through dot voting will help the team narrow in on problems worth addressing through the innovation process.

As a team, set a deadline for a final decision to be made. Setting a final decision meeting will prevent your team from going around in circles if there is disagreement, and it will ensure that the team follows a timeline for moving forward. During the meeting, generate a comprehensive list of possible action areas on sticky notes and put them on a wall where everyone can see. Once they're all up, take a step back and reflect on them. Think about what it would mean for your organization to solve these problems. Think about what it would mean for the community. As you discuss within your team, begin to categorize the sticky notes and group the ideas using whatever parameters your team feels are appropriate—this can be grouping based on importance, feasibility, potential impact, relevance to your mission, the team's interest or excitement around the topic—the potential categories are endless. Your team will organically begin to narrow in on your action area as you deepen your discussion and shift the sticky notes around. You will soon begin to see areas of priority emerge visually because there will be notes that are consistently perceived as important.

Usually, having a simple team conversation leads you to selecting *the* problem your team wants to focus on. If coming to a final consensus still requires more work, have team members vote on their problem area of preference. Getting used to voting will be helpful because you'll be doing more of it during the *Innovate* phase.

After so much work and discussion, end on a high note. Once your team has decided on a problem and its framing, go back and do a final activity, one that imagines the impact the innovation project will have on the organization and its target population. This will get the team energized about the innovation process that lies ahead. One way of doing this is for the team to collectively create a mock agency newsletter highlighting the work done by the innovation team at the end of your innovation process. Have them imagine what the headline story might be at the end of their innovation project. Think of quotes, photo-ops, stats, and any other elements that will bring the team's success story to life. This is a good opportunity for your team to revisit the Root Cause Activity from the *Initiate* phase, discuss goals for the project, and suspend limitations as you consider what it will mean for your agency to address this social issue.

FRAME YOUR INITIAL PROBLEM

We will further discuss this later in the chapter, but, as you move forward, keep in mind that *the way you frame your problem matters*. To start off, frame your problem statement in a way that allows your team to do broad research on the topic. For example, maybe your team has identified your problem as "We need to increase contraception access to teens." Branch out to encompass a broader topic area. By doing so, you will be open to discovering new information and opportunities that will impact your understanding of the issue's root causes and will likely drive you to generate solutions with a larger impact.

Instead, you might shift your problem statement to something along the lines of "We want to improve safe sex among teens" or "We want to help teens make informed decisions about their sexual health." These problem statements allow you to get at the core of what your team is hoping to address, but it also opens the doors to discovering new information that can significantly influence the direction you take.

Your problem statement is *not* static. It will change and evolve depending on new information that you discover through your research of the problem. Consider target population, location, scope of issue, and timeframe when formulating your initial problem statement. Your initial problem should spark curiosity and allow the team to delve into research areas relevant to the issue at hand. At this point in the innovation process, consider your problem statement to be a guiding light toward understanding the problem rather than a specific final destination. You'll be doing plenty of course correction along the way.

Monster Activity

1. If your social problem were a monster, what would it be like? As a team, create a monster that describes your problem. Think about its strengths, its weaknesses, where it lives, what it does on a daily basis, and its reasons for doing such things. Describe the monster's life and how it came to be the monster that it is. Paint a vivid picture and be visual and descriptive.
2. In the world that your monster lives in, what character does your organization embody? How do these two characters interact with each other, and what kinds of influences do you have on one another?
3. Use this fictitious interaction to generate a problem statement in a couple sentences.

Developing your problem into a character will help you shed new light on the problem by looking at it from an abstract perspective. You can make the most of this activity by asking the right questions. Have them prepared ahead of time. Have additional probes in case the team has a difficult time using their imagination. Consider your organization's mission, goals, vision and culture and how it aligns with the social problem you aim to address. What would it mean for your organization and stakeholders to tackle this monster? Don't forget to discuss unknown aspects of the monster that remain in the shadows. They will be helpful for you as you research your issue more in depth.

DIVE DEEP INTO THE ISSUE

Once you have honed in on your issue, it's time to know it inside and out. Consider this *Investigate* phase as an opportunity to see the problem with new eyes and incorporate a beginner's mindset as described in Chapter 3. This is a chance to be proactive about learning from other perspectives, challenging your assumptions, and questioning what's already being done. Through an empathic inquiry process, we not only see the problem as we understand it, but also through the eyes of others. Approach problems with the fresh mind of a beginner in order to allow yourself the space to ask questions and genuinely listen and learn from responses.

The idea is not to develop solutions at this point, but rather to ask and answer as many questions as possible about the problem at hand. When you know the problem and all the factors at play, it will be that much easier and more natural to develop solutions to address the causes perpetuating the problem. Be open to where the research takes you. You will likely be surprised or moved by your findings. That's great! When this happens, allow your findings to speak for themselves and guide the next set of questions or activities.

The guidelines in this section will help you identify which research strategies will be useful for your team. Some are tried-and-true research strategies. Some are likely to be new strategies you haven't come across. Identify what fits your problem and your team. Don't be afraid to try something new and make some mistakes. Innovation is about trying, failing, learning, and trying again.

LEARN FROM CREATIVE MINDS

There's already a lot of inspiring work being done in the field of social innovation—this is likely to be the case within your specific focus, too. A good place to begin now that your team has identified the problem you will be addressing is to draw inspiration from what's already out there. Discovering existing innovations can help you in your own innovation journey. This is an opportunity for you to be inspired by new ideas, learn from their successes and challenges, and unlock new ways of thinking. From processes and products to policies and enterprises, the social innovation world is a large one. Looking at different interventions that have already been designed can spark new ways of looking at your social problem.

In social innovation, we aim to build on the ideas of others—that includes people who are outside of your innovation team, too. As you begin to research your social problem, you will without a doubt come across some very exciting ideas being implemented in the social sector and beyond. Use them to your advantage! The ideas you discover don't necessarily have to directly translate into a solution for your defined problem in order for them to be influential in your own innovation process. Sometimes you may be inspired by the way an intervention uses color to express an idea, other times you may be inspired by a creative strategy used to engage the community in the development of the project. Whatever it is about the innovation that has inspired you, make a note of it and continue to tap into it as a resource for helping you think outside the box. Share these innovations with your team and keep track of these interventions. They may be particularly helpful to you during your team's ideation.

There are many ways to discover what's already being done. An obvious yet important starting point is a web search. The Internet is overflowing with great ideas (and not so great ideas, too, so be careful!). To see new ideas that are just emerging, take a look at popular crowdfunding platforms like Indiegogo, Kickstarter, and GoFundMe. You can also search nonprofits whose mission aligns with your own. If you want to learn more about a particular program or process, reach out to the organization. If you want to learn even more, invite someone from the organization to have an informal phone or in-person meeting with your innovation team. Looking at existing solutions may support a deeper or different understanding of the problem your team has identified.

LOOK AT THE LITERATURE

Begin to strengthen your expertise in your problem area by looking at the relevant literature. This can help you discover new advances made in the field, learn about significant academic studies that have emerged, and understand contrasting viewpoints on your social issue. As a team, brainstorm any major questions you might have about your social problem and figure out what each person will be researching and how you will share this information. Use the following questions to start your research:

- What is the history and scope of this issue in the community? In our field of practice?
- What interventions have been particularly impactful?
- How has technology been used to address this problem?
- Has this issue existed in other places? What have they done to address it?
- What interventions have been discontinued and why?
- Why has there been little progress made on this issue?

Don't feel like you have to read every academic article that has been written on the topic. Skim through the ones that seem promising, and take the time to read them in more detail if they seem interesting. If there is an article that you found particularly helpful, take a look at other things written by the author or the sources being cited. The further you dig, the more informed your innovation will be. A literature search can also help your team be informed of brand-new advances being made in the field that may have been previously unknown to them.

In addition to helping you become an expert in this social issue, this step will also help support your argument with particularly salient research from the field. Often, the social problem we are addressing in the field is very clear to nonprofit workers but less so to those outside our circles. Having a landscape of the literature and relevant data will help build the case for action when presented to others, such as potential funders, local government representatives, and potential corporate partners.

HIT THE GROUND RUNNING: NEW AND TRADITIONAL FIELD RESEARCH METHODS

To understand your problem in a robust way, it's important to take on various research strategies. This will enrich your understanding of the issue and help ensure that the solutions that are later generated are grounded on solid data. When you engage in different forms of field research, you deepen your insight into the problem. You break out of the habit of seeing the issue through your specific lens and understand the problem from the perspective of the users. Often, the key insights unlocked through field research allow us to more readily see the root cause of the issue, thus giving us the opportunity to develop solutions with significant impact. Even if your team already has expertise in the area you're aiming to address, information collected from field research can be helpful for informing others of the issue at hand.

The types of research that your team can engage in are endless. In this section, we provide a mix of methods that incorporate both traditional methods that the nonprofit field has always embraced along with newer approaches that have been borrowed from other fields. Try whichever make sense for your team and your identified problem. This is in no way a prescriptive set of activities. Rather, they are suggestions to get you thinking outside the box and curious about the many ways in which you can discover meaningful insights.

Think about the questions your team has about the social issue and how these research methods can be utilized to get some answers. When selecting the field methods you will be engaging in, make sure everyone has a role and a plan for communication. Not everyone can or should attend an interview, for example, but it is important that everyone have access to the information gathered from the interview. Recordings and summaries of your research activities can go a long way. However your team decides to move forward, try to ensure that your approach be as collaborative, communicative, and high-spirited as possible. Remember that many of the activities are purposefully meant to be light-hearted, so keep the innovation process feeling, fun, interesting, and engaging.

Tools for Rethinking Assessment

1. Interview stakeholders
2. Search for positive deviance
3. Map
4. Predict the future
5. Conduct focus groups
6. Immerse yourself
7. Ask through surveys
8. Develop a simulation
9. Analyze the competition
10. Externalize the problem
11. Use creativity for new understanding

INTERVIEW STAKEHOLDERS

We've been conducting interviews since the beginning of the field and for a very good reason—because it's an effective way of getting information! Reflect on what you don't know but need to know and brainstorm a list of people who have access to that information. Organize a list of questions and reach out to them. If you can record the interview, the information can be shared with team members who aren't present.

SEARCH FOR POSITIVE DEVIANCE

In any given situation, there typically exist outliers who defy the norm. People who have made it despite the presence of limiting circumstances. It may be a family who has healthy eating habits even though they live in a food desert. It may be a standout school that has an exceptionally high level of parental engagement. Whatever the context may be, identify those outliers and discover what makes them tick. Their skills and strategies can shed incredible insight on how to do things differently from the mainstream.

MAP

With technology being more accessible than ever, we are able to integrate it into our work in cost-effective ways. Geographic information system (GIS) mapping allows us to view the problem visually on a map and overlay it with other social factors to assess prevalence and correlation. The information shared through the US Census is widely available to use, and platforms for manipulating these data can be easily accessed on computers and tablets. If you do not have access to more sophisticated mapping, use what you can find to examine locations and distance. If the information you're looking for isn't there, it's very feasible for your team to go out to capture the information yourselves!

PREDICT THE FUTURE

Although your team may not have a crystal ball with which to see the future, pretending as though you do can actually be helpful. Looking at current trends can help you identify what is likely to happen in the future. Having an informed guess as to what the future may hold can help you prepare possible responses to those scenarios. Think about trends that are likely to have a significant impact on your social issue. If you're looking at providing services for the elderly, acknowledging and thinking through future trends such as medical advances, population growth, and influential policies can greatly impact the solutions you generate. Consider engaging in a Delphi method approach, in which you consult with experts to debate and accurately forecast the future of your social problem.

CONDUCT FOCUS GROUPS

Focus groups have been a tried-and-true way of obtaining rich information from various stakeholder groups. With a few targeted questions and representation of key stakeholders, your team can capture lots of rich information that can help you both gain insight on some questions and generate new questions for further exploration. Pay particular attention to the people at the table, how you get them there, and how you set the stage. Helping people feel comfortable and explaining the potential impact of their contribution can improve the quality of the information shared.

IMMERSE YOURSELF

There's nothing like seeing a situation first-hand. Enter a space to observe the situation for yourself and gain empathy for the users. If you're looking to address the issue of public transit in your community, no amount of pictures, stories, or readings can shed the same level of insight as replacing your car with the local bus for the week. Going through the same motions as your target population will unveil new perspectives and will allow you to see things that you previously overlooked. If you're interested in doing something different, try immersing yourself in a parallel situation. For example, if you are having issues in your nonprofit's waiting area, immerse yourself in similar spaces, such as the waiting area of a doctor's office or a line at a museum. See how things are done differently and how this might help inform what you're doing.

ASK THROUGH SURVEYS

If you want to capture a lot of data in a short time, surveys might be the way to go. Figure out the questions your team would like answered and develop them into a brief, yet informative survey. Often, this quantitative data can be particularly persuasive when discussing your issue with people of high rank within your agency, funders, and public officials. Thanks to email and social media, you can reach an even broader audience. Be sure to test your survey before sending it out.

DEVELOP A SIMULATION

Fire drills were a part of your childhood for a reason. Simulated events can help shed insight on how people will respond in a particular situation. Though it may only be appropriate in some contexts, simulation can allow you to see where gaps exist in response and can allow you to guess how a situation might play out in real life. If your organization would like to develop a know-your-rights curriculum, it might be helpful to develop a simulated situation where they are expected to interact with authority to see what people already know about their rights and what additional information might be beneficial.

ANALYZE THE COMPETITION

The business field does this quite well, and we can learn a thing or two from it. When we analyze the competition, we get a general landscape of the strengths and needs in the field. We discover possible alliances and reflect on how we can strengthen what our agency already does. It's not often that we take a step back to assess barriers and connectors across a particular issue. If you're looking to innovate for the immigrant community, for example, it's important to know what people are already doing, how they're doing it, and how effective they are. Network analysis and stakeholder mapping are other useful tools that can help your team take a step back and analyze a situation from a macro perspective.

EXTERNALIZE THE PROBLEM

The mental health field has embraced the concept of personifying problems in order to externalize an issue and see it as separate from the person. Similarly, we can utilize this approach to help us look at a social issue as separate from the organization. By giving us this distance, we can take a more objective look at how the issue is developing and the impact that it is having on the community. Exercises like the Monster Activity help your team do just that by externalizing the problem.

USE CREATIVITY FOR NEW UNDERSTANDING

We have often focused on creativity as a way to unleash new understanding and engage different people. To understand the problem, this approach also works well. It helps engage those who may be less vocal or otherwise reticent to speak up. It allows participation from those who may not be able to express their ideas due to language barriers. It distributes power and idea sharing in a more equitable manner, as drawing often puts people on the same playing field. And it uses a different part of the brain, allowing new thoughts to flow. Creative approaches can involve drawing, videotaping, or creating pictorial representations of the problem. The A Day in the Life Activity is one approach that can get people thinking about the user and problem by utilizing creativity.

A Day in the Life Activity

1. As a team, imagine your typical user and draw them on a flip chart or dry erase board. Be thorough in your description and consider their name, age, where they live, what they do for a living, when they were first exposed to the problem, what they do to cope with it, and the like. Be as complete and visual as possible.
2. Identify a few scenarios in which this user is exposed to the problem. Again, be visual and draw these scenarios so everyone can see.
3. Break off into small groups and have each group take one of the scenarios identified and imagine what the user's day is like when experiencing that situation.
4. Have the groups share their stories with each other and discuss.

When we try to envision the problem from the perspective of the user, often we see things in a new light. The user's experience with the issue is often multifaceted, and, by imagining various scenarios where the user is interacting with the problem, we can identify new problem areas or possible opportunities for intervention. Because we often serve a diverse community, it might be helpful to try this activity with a variety of users and compare the different stories that result. Bring a careful eye to ensure that the users identified are nuanced and reflect the population to prevent the activity from perpetuating stereotypes.

When you research your social issue through varied techniques, you allow yourself to take an objective look at the problem and its influencing factors. Doing so allows you to uncover new perspectives and challenge your assumptions. The combination of different research techniques helps you gain greater empathy for your target population, which, in addition to simply being important, will become particularly relevant when designing solutions that are sensitive to the users' lived experience. This emphasis on truly understanding the social problem and the target population is the strength of innovation within the nonprofit sector because nonprofits share a commitment to designing interventions that are based on both evidence and empathy.

SYNTHESIZE YOUR INSIGHTS

Whether you've sent out a survey to 100 people or you've conducted focus groups with 10, field research always turns out loads of data. Making the most out of this information is the next challenge for you and your team. This is an opportunity for the team to share with each other the lessons each has gleaned from various research activities. Since presumably not everyone has participated in all the activities, organizing and sharing research findings will be important for keeping everyone well-informed.

Some of the research findings will support your initial hypothesis and will validate your problem statement. On the other hand, some of your research might challenge your teams' assumptions and bring about new insights. Both are important for understanding the problem, and both are important for demonstrating the need for action. Remember that you are learners in a social context that is constantly evolving, so it's only natural that new insights should surface. Use these insights to rethink your problem, even if it means starting over.

Go through your different research strategies and extract the most significant findings. What did you find that was unexpected? What questions have been left unanswered? What was the most emotionally compelling interaction? What are the most prominent themes and priorities that have emerged? What have been the most persuasive quotes and figures discovered? The questions you ask will enrich the conclusions you are able to draw. The more targeted your questions, the more meaning you will get out of the research your team has done. The Superhero Activity gives you one approach to synthesize and discuss what you have learned.

Superhero Activity

1. For this activity, your team will assume the identity of a superhero. The group should come up with a name that represents the team or organization.
2. Explain that throughout the research your team has conducted, you have developed super powers. Using this activity, the team will see how their new super powers will be useful in better responding to the problem.
3. Set up six flip charts around the room, each depicting one of your superpowers.
   • *Strength*: What are existing strengths and resources in the community?

- *Hearing*: What did you hear the community saying about the problem?
- *Healing*: What previous challenges has the community overcome?
- *X-ray vision*: What did you see during your research that you previously could not see?
- *Super speed*: Why is it critical to act quickly on this issue?
- *Kryptonite*: What are the major barriers facing solution generation?
4. Divide into pairs and fill out each of the flip charts using words or images. When completed, present each of the super powers to the team.

Once everyone has presented, discuss the significance of your research findings on how you interpret the identified problem. Discuss insights, surprises, and figures that may confirm previous suspicions. If you would like to go a step further, discuss how your super powers can help you identify the arch nemesis (the problem) and the arch nemesis' characteristics. What will be important to defeat the nemesis?

In addition to drawing greater insight on the issue as a team, field research findings are critical for drawing support for your innovation process. Having concrete data to support your argument will amplify your credibility when it comes to expressing the need for action. When people, including stakeholders or leaders within the organization, are presented with evidence, they become more receptive to the issue and will recognize the need for action. In this way, it is not just the team that is saying there is a need for action, but rather it's the evidence speaking for itself!

(RE)DEFINE YOUR PROBLEM STATEMENT

Because we are guided by our findings and not our assumptions, the way we conceptualize our problem is likely to change throughout the course of the *Investigate* phase. New ways of looking at a problem and unearthing information that was previously unknown to us makes it natural for us to reframe the way we look at a social issue. While looking at the problem of youth employment, for example, your team may have discovered barriers to employment that you weren't previously unaware of or new resources in the community that could make for strong partnerships. Through this process of assessing and reassessing the social issue by means of your research, your team will be able to home in on service gaps that exist within the community. This will allow you to prepare for ideation by having a solid understanding of the root causes of your issue.

As you finalize your problem statement, make sure everyone's priorities are aligned. That means that the innovation team has identified a priority that reflects both the agency's mission and the community's goals. Making clear the alignment between various stakeholder groups will not only demonstrate that your team is being inclusive of diverse perspectives, but it will also promote collaboration and produce a less top-down approach.

The way you frame your problem will have significant implications in the innovation process. As with other elements of the innovation process, the more you practice properly framing problems, the better you get. There is no magic formula: sometimes the way a problem is framed just "feels right." Dedicate time to framing it correctly—this will go a long way. Your problem statement should be open enough to allow you to generate a variety of ideas and not orient you to an obvious solution. At the same time, your problem statement should be narrow enough to provide a clear direction for your team during your ideation phase. Aspects of your problem framing that can help you narrow in or broaden your framing include target population, location, scope of issue, and timeframe.

An example might be best for describing how to strike a balance in problem framing. Suppose you are an agency working in the field of homelessness and would like to use the innovation process to improve the physical health of women served by your organization. After some research, your team has identified the prevalence of untreated diabetes as the main priority area. The next steps you take in framing your problem will significantly impact the solutions you generate. For example, if your problem statement is "Women experiencing homelessness need more access to diabetes treatment," then the solution becomes obvious—provide more medical treatment. On the other hand, saying something along the lines of, "Our agency is not doing enough to improve women's health," is not solution-focused and is also too broad. So how do we strike a balance? Much of it will depend on your team and your goals. In this example, a problem statement that says, "How can we facilitate the process for women experiencing homelessness to manage their diabetes?" can yield a variety of solutions. Utilize the problem statement activity to capture the team's current thinking on the problem.

Problem Statement Activity

Use the following tool to develop and refine your problem statement. Make sure you are checking each element and making corrections as needed.
  Identify the Problem:

1. Write your initial problem statement prior to your research.
2. Discuss the following topics:
    What is the social problem you are addressing?
       a. Make sure there is a problem stated clearly that reflects what you learned in the literature.
    Who is the target population being affected?
       b. Clear description of population affected.
       c. Population target is limited in scope and geography.
    Does your statement already reflect a specific solution?
       d. Statement does not already reflect a specific solution.
    Does your organization's mission, goals, visions, and culture align with your understanding of the problem?

    e. Statement does align with organizational goals, mission, and culture.

    f. If it does not align, is there a reason for this? Is it possible that the organization might want to go in this new direction?

   Why does this problem matter?

    g. Be clear about why this problem matters.

3. Rewrite your problem statement after research and consideration of the problem statement tool.

Having a purposeful space to discuss the trajectory of the problem will be useful for your team because you can organize your data and assess the way in which your thought patterns have evolved. Deciding on proper framing of the problem will greatly facilitate solution generation, so don't be afraid to spend some extra time to get it just right.

CONVEY YOUR PROBLEM

Because your team is part of a larger organization and a broader community of vested stakeholders, getting others to share in your mission to address this problem is an ongoing and instrumental part of the process. Social innovation is not a solitary endeavor—the more people you have supporting your team, the more resources you will have to launch and sustain your innovation.

Begin by sharing the most significant findings with people who are already interested in what you're doing. Amplify your voice by identifying those who are already likely to agree with you. Get them to be active advocates of your team's goals and why it's important to act on this issue. Building support for your cause early on is certain to pay off during the implementation of your innovation.

Think about your most compelling findings. Utilize stories, quotes, facts, and figures to convey your work to leaders in your organization. Let them know not only why you've identified this as an issue, but also the opportunities that could result from addressing this. How can targeting this issue help the organization further its mission? Make connections clear between the problem identified, your organization's mission, and its current programs. Your problem statement should be something that complements your current work by addressing service gaps. Remember that, in addition to this being a problem that your team has identified, this is an opportunity for your organization to spark change.

REFLECTION ON INVESTIGATING FROM WITHIN

1. Considering the time you will need to invest in this stage of the innovation process, how might you face time restrictions of balancing the fieldwork with the

rest of the team's responsibilities? What are the organizational characteristics that might help or hinder this part of the process?

2. What have been the most significant experiences that you and your team experienced while investigating? How might you share the impact and meaning of these aha moments with the rest of the staff and stakeholders?

3. How has your concept of empathy changed throughout your fieldwork?

MAIN POINTS FOR INVESTIGATING FROM WITHIN

- By taking an introspective look at the problems and opportunities surrounding the organization, innovation teams can identify areas where they want to take action. These can be emerging social issues, gaps in current services, or a desire to integrate new technologies.
- Set deadlines for identifying problem statements to ensure the team is moving forward—having different perspectives at the table might make it difficult for people to agree on an action area. Discussion and voting will be helpful when selecting the action area for your team.
- A literature review will turn up lots of new information on your issue, including new advances in the field and strategies that are being done elsewhere. Use this as a platform to start.
- Field research will yield rich insights that will help your team develop solutions that are well-informed and reflect the expressed needs of various stakeholders. The quantitative and qualitative information discovered will be critical for getting others on board.
- The way you frame your problem will have significant implications on the way your team generates solutions. A problem that is too narrow will point to an obvious solution, while a well-framed problem statement will allow your team to generate a broad range of solutions.
- Start sharing the problem with others in the organization for early buy-in that this issue must be solved.

INNOVATE

Chapter 6 provides a burst of creativity through tips and activities to help you and your team ideate innovative and sustainable solutions.

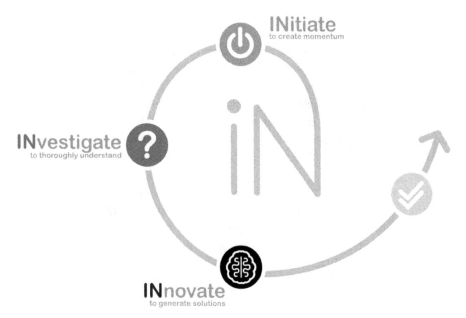

FIGURE 6.1: Innovate model.

Get ready to ...

1. Ideate wild (and realistic) solutions to your problem.
2. Develop and test several prototypes with stakeholders in the field.
3. Share and receive feedback to refine your solution.

The road ahead for you and your team is exciting, challenging, demanding, and gratifying. It's an opportunity to develop solutions that will have meaningful and lasting impact on the communities you work with. The innovation process will make it possible for your team to take a new, fresh approach to tackle the questions and concerns that arose for you during your research. This is the time for you to tap into your creativity and test solutions you believe have the potential to enrich your organization's work.

When we ideate solutions, we borrow from sectors like design, which take a creative approach to solving problems—knowing that creativity is necessary to approach problems in a different, more effective manner. When we prototype solutions, we borrow from the engineering sector, where testing iterations of your solution helps you tweak and modify your solution until you have the product you're looking for. When we use these particular strategies from various sectors and integrate them into our work within nonprofits, we are adopting a calculated risk approach often used in business. By collecting data and testing our solutions, we use qualitative and quantitative mathematical approaches to minimize the risk involved in launching a new innovation.

Nonprofits have legitimate reasons to be cautious about risk—they are making changes that impact the lives of people, failure can have implications for the lives and communities that relate to their mission, their financial structures often dissuade risk, and the payoff to risk may seem less clear than in business. But nonprofits need risk—calculated, purposeful risk—to develop the best programs, services, and products to solve pressing issues. Using an innovation process that allows for data, testing, and feedback mitigates risk and allows us to launch new solutions with greater confidence. We borrow and adapt approaches from other fields to make the work we do stronger. Some of these strategies may be new, some may be familiar. *Innovate* will help you leverage those strategies (Figure 6.1).

As you progress through this chapter, you will accomplish three things: generate a solution, refine it through various steps, and test it in the field. Each step is purposeful in its way of guiding your team through the many essential tasks in the innovation process (Figure 6.2).

We are not just ideating for the sake of developing an income-generating product, as might be the case in the for-profit sector; we are innovating to purposefully design more efficient, more effective solutions for the populations we serve. *Innovation from within* requires particular attention to our realities as nonprofits. When innovating, we must be aware of the sociopolitical context, the stakeholders at play, available resources, and the potential for social impact—among countless other things, of course. The process of

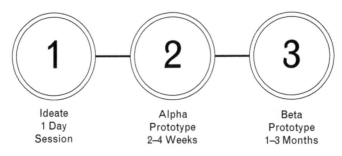

FIGURE 6.2: Innovation timeline.

innovation that we go through as nonprofits must take into account and integrate this context into the way innovations are developed. It's an ambitious feat, but innovation requires nothing less, so let's get started.

IDEATE SOLUTIONS FROM WITHIN

If the thought of developing new, creative solutions to your problem seems daunting—after all, your agency has been engaged with these complex issues for a long time—here is some good news: it's easier than you think. Now that you have done your research, you have a keen awareness of the existing services, problems, and opportunities specifically related to the issue you're looking at. This will help ideas flow as you and your team try to generate fresh solutions. Once you're familiar with the innovation process and its activities, you will be surprised by the ease of the process and the wealth of ideas generated by the team. Each time you go through the innovation process, it becomes more natural and results in stronger ideas.

While the ideas you come up with may not always be completely "new," you will find new ways of looking at the issue, new applications of existing solutions, and new ways to adapt an exciting solution that is already out there. Ideating new solutions is about unleashing the potential for solutions that respond to your issue in a way that is more effective or more efficient than previous interventions.

As you gear up for innovation, there are a few things to keep in mind. As we mentioned in Chapter 3 and Chapter 4, your team must be ready for innovation. A mindset that is curious, collaborative, and receptive is necessary for ideating and giving and receiving feedback. Be purposeful about integrating the right conditions for innovation before launching your team into a brainstorming session. Have supplies on hand that stimulate different kinds of thinking and open the group up to new ideas. If you have a discussion about failing valiantly, for example, write it onto large butcher-block paper and post it up in your workspace to remind the team that failing and learning from failure is an unavoidable and important part of the process.

More so than in other parts of the innovation process, the *Innovate* phase is particularly fast-paced. This is the case for many reasons. First, we don't want the team to become idea-stagnant. Creative juices should keep flowing continually throughout your ideation process. When we're given too much time to think, we stop focusing on the task at hand and our mind begins to wander. When we have too much time, we pay too much attention to the barriers to implementation rather than being open to wild, creative new ideas. Instead, short time limits on activities keep new ideas pouring in and participants engaged. Think back to a time when you wish you had another minute to work on something. There is excitement and energy that is propelling you forward. If only for another minute, you would love to continue working on your project. This is precisely the momentum you want to capture during your ideation sessions.

Timing is just one of the magic elements that ignite ideation sessions. To bolster the energy of the room, consider other components that contribute to the overall feel of the session. Space. Materials. Food. Background music. The environment your team inhabits should foster the creativity and outcomes you're looking to generate. Your workspace has ripple effects on your process and end results.

Last, but not least, check in on your team's confidence level. How is everyone doing? What kind of encouragement is needed for the team to move forward? Innovation might be new territory for the team, which sometimes translates into insecurity or fear. If that's the case, give the team a brief overview of the process you will use to generate new solutions. Remind the team that this is an area where nonprofits have long-standing expertise. We have a long history of working effectively with communities, seeing social issues in a new light, and acting on those through a social justice lens. This is no different. The process for innovation will help the team take a critical look at the issue and utilize various opportunities at our disposal to create sustainable change.

STEAL OUTSIDE IDEAS

Before sitting down with your team to generate ideas, look outward. There are many great ideas already floating around. Why not take advantage of them? Idea generation can be strengthened through teamwork and building on the ideas of others. So, look at ideas that already exist in the field and see how and if they might be useful to your own innovation process. This, however, does not mean your team simply applies someone else's solution; rather, you can adapt and use parts of existing ideas to create the type of innovative solutions that fit your organization and context.

Thanks to new technologies, the ideas of thousands of people are at our disposal. If a team of 10 people can generate great ideas, imagine what a group of 100 or 1,000 could do. Utilizing the concept of open innovation, we can harness the power of crowds to generate solutions. Platforms such as One Billion Minds, IdeaConnection, and Ideaken allow us to pitch a problem to a broad audience and listen to their response. Complete and partial solutions can be derived from this process. New ideas and new considerations can be sparked. Adapting others solutions for your population and community becomes possible. Connections can be formed between what your team is trying to address and actions being taken in the broader community. Open innovation allows you to get ideas from the many people out there who are also interested in your work.

A similar type of open innovation activity can be replicated within your own workplace. Consider developing ways for colleagues, clients, board members, or external stakeholders to contribute ideas. This can be a way for many stakeholders to be a part of the innovation process. The level of involvement can be up to you. Do you want to keep it simple and facilitate a quick ideation session during a staff meeting? Would you like to do something more involved and have staff members vote on their favorite ideas and offer a reward? Nonprofits have the possibility to develop ongoing calls for ideas through competitions, suggestion boxes, or open innovation platforms for submitting ideas on an ongoing basis. Take this idea and make it your own. Keep in mind that the more involved people feel in the innovation process, the more connected they will feel to the final solution and implementation.

Inviting others into the ideation process is a win-win situation. For the team, you get many brains working collaboratively to solve the issue you care about. While it may or may not give you *the* winning solution, open innovation will give you many considerations as you continue your solution generation process. On the other hand, participants in open innovation also benefit. It also builds greater awareness of the challenges at hand. It's an opportunity to discuss challenges and solutions with others, share ideas on social media, and link to a community that cares about the same values. More importantly, it allows people to feel they are a part of solving the social issue they care so deeply about.

You also have the opportunity to draw inspiration from the innovations you came across during your research. Have your team share their list of inspiring innovations. What is it about these ideas that make them exciting? Is it the way in which organizations collaborate with others? Is it the way in which they incorporate technology? Maybe it's the smart business model that they've adopted. Compile and reflect on what makes these ideas great. Some of these elements can help you imagine new possibilities for your own solution generation.

Remember that you can also find inspiration from areas that are seemingly dissimilar from your field. If your organization is interested in designing an advocacy day, for example, you might want to look at what college campuses are doing to mobilize students. In the same vein, you could even look at what the latest podcast is doing to reach new audiences. Learning from the way others do things can really enhance your own efforts—even if it seems like you have nothing in common with the other organizations. Benchmarking is a traditional approach to comparing your own processes, strategies, and performance to industry best practices. In addition to comparing to successes in your own area, find out who excels outside your specific area or even outside the sector. Comparing to leaders in the sector can help you move beyond others in your space. There is plenty to learn from the ways other fields work and, particularly, from those who have demonstrated excellence.

READY THE TEAM

Excitement is high. This is the time that you'll finally come up with that solution your team has been looking forward to. Considering all the time and energy spent on readying your organization, selecting your team, and conducting field research, it's surprising to think that the solution generation phase can happen all in one day or in a short-term format—but that's the case! Quick, focused ideation sessions can guide a team toward the first version of the ultimate solution. Be prepared for the day and ensure that everyone will be in attendance, you have all materials, and that you've gone out of your way to set the right tone. Everything that you have been doing up until this moment has been preparing you for this day—or concentrated set of events—to ideate in a fast-paced manner that is engaging, relevant, and socially informed. On this day, you have three objectives: ready the team, ideate, and pick a winner. Don't worry; we'll help guide you through these.

In much the same way that you don't start a race without first stretching, you want to make sure to begin the day with some excitement and some creativity stretches. Following the same logic, you're not likely to be the best runner from day 1, so the more practice you and your team can have in ideation prior to diving into the solution of your problem the better.

To prepare your team for a day of original thinking, start off with a game. We suggest starting off with our Problem Solvers Activity, but there are plenty of others you could also include in your day. Look into the Marshmallow Challenge (2014) for a fun (and learning-filled) competition or hold a quick cartoon caption contest among the group. These activities could also serve as energy boosts or fun breaks throughout the day.

You also want to prime your team with creativity, prime your team with inspiration by exposing them to a wealth of possibilities for innovation. What we find with many nonprofits—especially when it's their first time engaging in the innovation process—is that they have a difficult time thinking outside of the box. Solutions tend to be similar to the programs already established within the organization, or they might lack the vision to truly push the boundaries of social services. To remedy this, we suggest exposing the team to various structures of innovation, such as applications, products, social enterprises, gamified solutions, policies, and the like. Look back at Chapter 1 and review with your team some of the examples described so that they are already thinking outside the box when they ideate solutions.

Problem Solvers Activity

1. Prep the participants by explaining the activity and its purpose. It can be helpful to have a quick brainstorm session or conversation about the variety of possible solutions in innovation.
2. Break off into pairs and have each person describe to their partner a problem they have faced this week. The problem can be absolutely anything, but each person has only 7 minutes to describe the situation.
3. Allow 8 minutes for participants to ideate as many solutions as possible that will address the issue their partner described. It can be anything, including apps, products, art, a policy, a gamified solution, or the like. The goal is to generate *many* solutions—and quickly!
4. Next, each partner has an additional 7 minutes to describe their solutions and receive feedback.
5. Have everyone go back to the solutions they developed and, in 10 minutes, draw their top three solutions based on the feedback they received.
6. End by having each person share the three solutions with their partner. As a group, share some of the successful and not-so-successful solutions. Discuss the learning opportunities that came out of the activity.

This activity will help team members understand some of the key elements of innovation, including creativity, rapid prototyping, obtaining user feedback, time constraints, and failure. Talk about what worked and what didn't work and how these elements of innovation played out in the activity. You can also discuss the idea that some of the solutions developed are likely to address a specific issue, whereas others might be more abstract and tackle the root cause of the issue presented. Use this as an opportunity to prep team members to think of a broad range of solutions and to recognize that team members will come to the innovation activities with diverse experiential, cultural, and intellectual capital. How was this reflected in the activity? The more we value these differences, the easier it will be to innovate.

TABLE 6.1: Innovation guidelines

What	Why	How
Anything goes	Ideation is about broadening your possibilities. You will worry about limitations later. At this point, you want to encourage *all* ideas.	Make it explicit! Remind the team that wild ideas can also be useful for creative problem solving.
Build on the ideas of others	We don't often have full ideas. We don't often have the best ideas. But sometimes one person can say something that will spark an idea in the next. Utilize that power.	Adopt a "Yes, and . . . " approach. If someone says "Let's develop an app for people to donate." The next person can say "Yes, and in that app we should include space for sponsors to advertise."
Use your research as a launch pad	Throughout your field work, you have uncovered many useful insights on your problem. This is a time to incorporate the lessons learned.	As a team, list key insights from your research. What are key elements that *must* be addressed in your solution? What existing gaps and opportunities exist that your team can address? Post these around the room.
Think broadly	Solutions can be big or small. They can take the form of a traditional nonprofit program or they can be products, which are typically derived from the engineering sector. Think outside the box.	Review innovations that incorporate new approaches. Public art. Apps. Social enterprises. Media campaigns. All are fair game. Use the InnoGrid activity in this section to push your team to come up with a range of solutions.

In addition to warming up, it can also be helpful to set some rules to innovate by. Use your warm-up activity to reflect on how these rules apply. Did someone create a funny cartoon caption based on what someone else said? Did someone do a particularly great job at tailoring her solution to her partner in the Problem Solvers Activity? These conversations make the rules for innovation come to life and drive the messages home. As you set the foundation for the day, keep in mind the innovation guidelines shown in Table 6.1.

There is a final guiding light that will be needed to start your ideation off in the right direction—setting goals for your innovation. Even more important than ground rules for ideation, establishing goals for your solution will help orient the team to the types of issues you want your innovation to address. Agree on a list of 3–5 goals that your team has for the innovation you develop. These goals will be guiding principles that your innovation should aim to address at its core. With these overall guidelines under your belt, your team is ready to move on to the exciting stuff: developing solutions!

BRAINSTORM THE (IM)POSSIBLE

Some people enjoy working independently. Some people enjoy team work. In the innovation process, we incorporate both. This happens so that people who prefer to work in one capacity or the other have the opportunity to thrive and share their ideas. By having many heads working together and independently, you get a larger, more diverse number of solutions being contributed to the mix. Remember that here what we really want is *quantity*. Throughout the process, you'll find it encouraging when someone comes up with an idea that's along the same track as yours and interesting when someone brings a diverse perspective that takes the group on an alternate path. You'll find it stimulating when an idea proposed by someone sparks another idea that gets the team moving. All of these sparks bring the team that much closer to finding the answer it's looking for.

Ideation is the free-flowing process of generating as many ideas as possible. To help channel the team's ideas and creativity, follow the activities proposed in this section. Mix and match them depending on what feels right for the team and the flow of the day. At this stage, no ideas are bad. In fact, we encourage you to think wildly! Grand ideas, radical ideas, unexpected ideas, unrealistic ideas, and even fragments of ideas—they're are all extremely useful in this process. Everyone on your team has something valuable to offer in this step, so make sure all ideas are heard.

Ideation Activity

1. For 7 (timed) minutes, have the team individually brainstorm *as many* solutions to the problem as possible. These can be complete ideas or elements of solutions that you think are important. Think BIG and go for quantity not quality! About 40% of your ideas should be entirely unusable. Write down each idea on a sticky note, using one note per idea.
2. After ideating individually, have people share their solutions with a partner. Each person should take the time to explain all of his or her ideas.
3. Between the two partners, cluster similar and/or duplicate ideas into groups. Group them by theme on a flip chart for ease of organization. Identify a few of the most exciting, innovative, and promising ideas for the pairs to share with the team. This should take 5–10 minutes.
4. Get together as a whole team, share, and discuss the top ideas shared by each pair. Everyone should have enough time to present his or her ideas. Instead of critiquing ideas, at this stage we're interested in building more and more. So, rather than critiquing, offer a "Yes, and . . . " comment after each pair presents.

The timeline for this task is intentionally short. Use time restraints to your advantage! Now is not the time to think too hard or overanalyze. The more quickly you move through this process, the less people will become attached to their own ideas, the more spontaneous their thoughts will be, and the more innovative your ideas will be! Ideas in this phase should be unpolished, grand, and do not have to be complete or focused. Encourage the team to think of as many solutions as they possibly can. Quantity is key during the initial ideation phase. The only requirement is that these ideas tackle the problem you're facing!

A common stumbling block for organizations is thinking outside the traditional non-profit box. On your own, you may think of lots of inventive new approaches, but within an organizational context people may feel constrained. To help allay this, we present activities to expand the team's thinking and explore past the ideas of a traditional nonprofit program. While this may not guide the ultimate solution, it may support new thinking about potential solutions to the issue. Even though at this point teams should be familiar with concepts like social enterprise, mobile technology, and gamification, it's helpful to review them before starting ideation day so that these innovative concepts are at the forefront.

InnoGrid Activity

1. Divide the team into groups of three and hand each group the grid shown in Table 6.2.

If our innovation had to be a(n)...

TABLE 6.2: InnoGrid

1	Tech-based solution	
2	Multiagency partnership (nonprofit or for-profit)	
3	Social enterprise	
4	Organizational or public policy	
5	Gamified solution	
6	Mobile app	
7	Social media–based solution	
8	Product	
9	Educational program	
10	Art-based solution	
Bonus:	If you had *unlimited* funding...	

2. Give the groups 3 minutes to respond to each number. After each number, have them share their best solution with the entire team.
3. Have everyone vote on their favorite response to the prompt. The team with the most votes by the end of the activity is the winner.

Get a feel for the team's pace. If 3 minutes is too long, shorten the time. If you think it's too little, give them a little more time. Depending on the problem your team is addressing, some prompts may not actually be possible. That's okay! The goal is to really stretch the way people think about how we can solve problems. The ideas, or elements of the ideas, that emerge from the activity can be combined to inform the final solution. If there are additional categories you want to add, feel free. Oh, and remember to find a good prize (or at least recognition) for the winning team!

While stand-alone ideas can be strong, sometimes it is the connections between the ideas that lead to the best solutions. Trying to find ways to combine or connect ideas often leads to more robust solutions.

Solutions Connector Activity

1. Select 6–10 ideas that the group finds to be the most promising and arrange them around the problem statement written on flip chart paper.
2. Often, ideas can complement each other and can be combined or modified to form stronger, more complex solutions. As a team, think of different ways that the ideas can form connections to complement each other.
3. Using a pen or a marker, draw a line from one idea to another to represent a connection. The connections formed can either represent a modified version of one of the solutions or a new idea all together. On the line drawn, briefly name or describe the new idea (using only a few words).
4. Once the team has formed as many connections as possible, take time to review as a group the ideas that have been formed.

What you're looking to do in this activity is to blend and build ideas. Sometimes your team comes up with part of an idea that could be complementary to another. This is a space to think about how you can compound ideas to create a more robust solution. As with several of the activities in this phase, it might be helpful if you guide your team through an example prior to having them do it on their own. Remember that, at this stage, they're still rough ideas!

By this point, your team will have generated many, many ideas—including, *the* winning idea you want to move forward. Next up, however, will be figuring out exactly which one it is. As you plunge into the next steps, though, make sure to document the innovation process your team has gone through so far. Take pictures, jot down reactions, store any ideas that the team has already eliminated. You want to keep a "parking lot" of ideas in case your team needs to go back to the drawing board at any time during the innovation process.

PICK A WINNER

Once you have a variety of ideas to choose from, the next priority for the team is to home in on a solution that makes the most sense for your identified problem. While ideation was grounded in the philosophy that more is better (big ideas and limitless opportunities), at this stage, teams must begin to analyze potential solutions by imposing practical constraints. Of the ideas generated, which would have the greatest impact? Which are the most promising? Exciting? Feasible? Which solutions are likely to have the greatest buy-in? The least buy-in? Which is viable, given your organization's current resources? What ideas best match with the organization's mission? Revisit the opportunities and challenges presented in Chapter 2 and use these to evaluate your solution. Encourage a conversation that will guide the team toward identifying the best possible solution.

For solution generation, games and creative activities go a long way. For selecting the right solution, however, we find that dedicating most of the time to open discussion works best. Have a time limit for how much time you will spend on selecting *the* right solution. Two hours, more or less, will be an appropriate time frame for a team to come to a consensus. A discussion without a clear deadline may result in a circular conversation. By the end of the discussion, your team should have picked the solution you will test through alpha prototyping. Remember that there will be opportunities to refine and adjust your solution, and there will always be an opportunity to go back to the drawing board. Your responsibility right now is to identify your best guess. Going from many solutions to a few lets you really explore solutions in depth so you can examine what works. Revisit the goals you established for your innovation and make sure that what you're discussing is in line with these goals. Keep in mind that many of the generated solutions are connected—grouping ideas and looking at sets of solutions might be helpful. Using connections between proposed ideas to come up with the winning solution may be the way to go.

After having narrowed in on the team's top solutions, use the Agency Fit Activity to have a concrete and visual way of qualifying the solutions. The activity will help the team recognize the various strengths and shortcomings of each proposed solution. Keep in mind that you don't have to limit yourselves to just one solution. If it's feasible for your team to launch multiple innovations or launch solutions in phases, why not? Any ideas that don't move forward can be put in a parking lot. Ideas placed in the parking lot can be revisited after prototyping. It could even be that the solutions you generate may not work for the organizational context at this time, but could work in the future given the right conditions, so keep them around and revisit them from time to time.

Agency Fit Activity

1. Distribute the chart in Table 6.3 to each team member.

TABLE 6.3: Agency fit

	Innovative	Practical	Addresses root cause	Feasible	Empathetic	Exciting	Embraces technology	Strengthens mission
Solution 1								
Solution 2								
Solution 3								
Solution 4								
Solution 5								

2. Collectively, agree on the team's top solutions and list them in the first column.
3. Individually, have each team member check off the measures they feel each solution fulfills.
4. Come together as a team and discuss findings and views.

There are many other possible measures to include in addition to those identified. Modify the chart based on what is relevant to your team. The activity makes the team consider parameters important for an effective innovation. Consider which of the measures are indispensable for your innovation to include and which are not as necessary. Can the solutions be modified to be more inclusive of the measures?

Sometimes there can be conflicting perspectives on which solution is best. If discussion does not lead to a solution agreed upon by most, your team can opt to have a formal vote. The team can vote by distributing three dots per person, then having them allocate the dots to whichever idea(s) they think are best. Alternatively, the team can have an anonymous vote and write their choices on a piece of paper. The team should also determine if there is anyone else who needs to weigh in or provide critical feedback at this time. Is it completely up to the team to decide? Does your team want to engage the community in selecting a winning idea? Do you need to receive approval from organizational leaders before moving forward? Would it be useful for the leadership to offer their opinions on your prospective solutions? How you do it is up to you, as long as it keeps the conversation moving forward in a positive, cohesive manner.

CREATE YOUR ALPHA PROTOTYPE

Your prototyping phase is an opportunity for your team to test your ideas with minimal risk. This step can be challenging in nonprofit work, but it can be instrumental for getting feedback to refine and improve your initial concept. Here, you will design an alpha prototype, which will allow you to convey your complete idea to others as a simple and inexpensive mock-up. In addition to helping you think through your concept in a comprehensive manner, your alpha prototype will allow you to fail cheaply and integrate the suggestions of people outside your innovation team. Your alpha prototype will be a simple mock-up or descriptor of your innovation that allows you to present your idea to others in order to receive their feedback. It will allow you to make changes without being so invested in the solution that you fail to see its weaknesses.

The alpha prototype is your opportunity to approximate or show a model of what you are proposing without investing significant resources in building or developing the real solution. It can be a sketch, a written description, or a 3-D version of the solution using easy-to-obtain materials. If you're designing an app, for example, instead of investing resources on designing an entire mobile platform, an alpha prototype suggests that you can instead draw it on paper as it would appear. If it's going to contain an introduction video, don't get a professional videographer to do it: use your cell phone and record something quick and easy.

This first draft will be something simple to show stakeholders a rough idea and get feedback from it. When we present the alpha prototype and ask for input, we invite the community to contribute to the solution as co-designers in further developing the solution. Are there key parts missing that you haven't thought of? Does the setup feel intuitive? Which components does the user find most useful? Your alpha prototype will help you and your team get answers to big-picture questions in a cost effective way.

Throughout the process, you will be zooming in and out of your proposed solution. You will first zoom in to figure out the details of what your innovation will actually look like. You will obtain feedback from within the team and from others. You will zoom out when you need to assess the strengths and shortcomings of your innovation. And you will zoom back in to make improvements. If you're going to make mistakes—which every innovation certainly does—this is the stage in which to do it. This is a low-risk stage where you can easily get input on your ideas and modify them without risking too many resources. Be open to feedback and be creative in your strategies for integrating outside opinions.

GO BACK TO THE DRAWING BOARD

To get to a point where you can receive feedback on your idea, your team must first come to an agreement on what your proposed solution will actually look like. Since the concept at this point might be vague, rough, or incomplete, you have to come together to figure out what the actual nuts and bolts of your innovation are. Use these steps to develop the full concept of your solution:

1. Talk through the solution as you now understand it.
2. Use visual materials—pictures, 3-D models to create a visual representation of your solution.
3. Use the fundamental six questions: *Who? What? Where? When? Why? How?* to make sure you are on the same page.
4. Create a tagline—a short phrase or sentence that captures the essence of your solution. Your tagline should be something that will leave a lasting memory when you pitch your idea to your stakeholders for feedback. Make it something short, catchy, and memorable.

As a facilitator, try to engage everyone in the process, whether it's by inviting them to verbalize suggestions or to record notes for the team. Use flip charts to document the process in a way everyone can see. Words, diagrams, charts, grids, and pictures can be effective—varying the visuals used will be helpful for bringing your idea to life and keep the process interesting. Be as detailed as possible in describing the functionality of your prototype and as clear as you can when developing the tagline to describe your solution.

As nonprofits, we have an obligation to go a step further during our prototyping process to ensure we are being mindful of the diverse needs of our communities. Issues of access, diversity, and cultural relevance are just as critical as issues of scalability and cost effectiveness. Devote as much time as needed to enhancing your alpha prototype through the lens of multiple perspectives. Be purposeful in designing a solution that is inclusive and mindful of the cultural assets of your community. By utilizing a user-centered design approach, we tailor the innovation to the user and thereby increase the relevance and effectiveness of the solution.

It's important to emphasize our obligation to be inclusive in the design. It's not merely enough to say all are welcome to participate in the innovation: we must be explicit about inviting diverse users to the table and intentionally making the innovation accessible to all. Many times, this means purposefully going out of the way to consider what you don't know you don't know. This is a concept we call "*right-handed pattern breaking*." When you go through life having everything designed specifically to meet your needs as a right-handed person—think chairs in a classroom, the number pad on a computer, the spirals on a notebook, etc.—you forget that these seemingly benign objects can present significant access hurdles to left-handed people. Unless we pause to consider how our innovations can be inclusive of as many users as possible, we will continue to inadvertently create barriers to access for people who are different from those who ideated the solution. Throughout the development of your innovation, consider any and all possible barriers to entry for historically marginalized groups such as people with disabilities, the LGBTQ community, women, economically poor people, and more, and develop plans that will prioritize their inclusion in your innovation.

Hearts and Haters Activity

1. Prepare for the activity by cutting out paper hearts, each representing one of the following personalities:
   - The Pessimist: Calls out everything that could go wrong with the solution
   - The Penny-pincher: Brings up all financial considerations that could arise
   - The Thoughtful: Challenges the inclusivity of the innovation: language, ability, age, gender, educational level, etc.
   - The Skeptic: Questions everything possible
   - The Optimist: Brings up "Yes, and. . . ." possibilities. Wants to add to what's already suggested
2. Stand in a circle and provide everyone with a heart. Each person is responsible for fulfilling the role assigned to them and will scrutinize the innovation based on their perspective. Go around the circle, sharing some comments from each person's perspective. It's up to the team to rectify any issue brought up by the personality sharing.

The key to the success of this activity is to have everyone assume his or her role as vigorously as possible. The more you think through these considerations now, the more prepared you will be in the future. If you're up for it, have fun with it and create full characters. This activity was adapted from the Six Thinking Hats Activity (De 1999), which can also be used by your team during this phase.

Through the process of building and refining, your team will identify some of the hurdles that lay ahead—and the strategies for dealing with them. If you have set a solid foundation among team members, everyone will feel comfortable verbalizing apprehensions or considerations for the proposed solution. This will greatly help your team and solution move forward. As you agree upon the details of your solution, develop the innovation into a visual representation to show others and update the solution's tagline. Preparing a visual will ready the team to pitch the solution to stakeholders for feedback, your next step. A visual will help you be concise and will help the person being asked better understand your proposed solution.

CALL IN THE EXPERTS

Your team is convinced this idea has potential—but how do others feel? When we work in isolated environments, an echo chamber of positive remarks often emerges. The cycle of positive feedback makes it difficult to see the solution and any possible shortcomings in an entirely objective manner. We can use exercises like the Hearts and Haters Activity to see other perspectives, but we also need to bring in outsiders. It makes sense that after an energizing ideation session and several hours working on building your idea, the team will be pretty excited about the solution developed. This momentum is great, but an outside perspective is particularly helpful at this point. Consider bringing in someone who can see the problem and solution with a fresh set of eyes and be able to share some insights that your team may have overlooked. Try to engage someone who has a different stake in solving the problem. Someone who has a different exposure or relationship to the problem. Who you decide to get feedback from and how you decide to collect it will have significant results on your final product.

Decide as a team which stakeholders you would like invite to provide feedback, how you would like to do it, and a reasonable timeline for you to finish and share lessons learned. Throughout the week or so, set up multiple interviews with these stakeholders. The more diverse your data, the better, as it will allow you to compare and contrast the feedback you receive. If your innovation is something that must be approved by your organization's management, this is a key time to get their input! You don't want to waste any additional resources going further if your agency's leadership is not on board. Even if it's not a requirement that you obtain approval, it is still valuable to integrate the leadership's feedback so they feel connected to your innovation process. Failing to develop a strong collaborative relationship with your agency's leadership can result in significant challenges during the implementation of your innovation.

Various stakeholders will be able to provide important feedback and critique during your refinement process. Consider engaging program recipients (a critical perspective!), potential donors, other coworkers, and colleagues from other agencies. The feedback does not have to be comprehensive or formal. At this point, your innovation isn't perfect, so an informal consultation can be enough. Just be sure to include a variety of perspectives. Brief interviews or meetings over coffee, a quick online survey, a focus group around your agency's lunch table—all are fair game for gathering people's responses to your proposed solution.

Many hands make light work, so divide the responsibility of obtaining feedback among the team and have each person share his or her findings with the team. Decide whether you would like to share information as it's gathered or if you would like to have one big share the next time you get together to redesign your prototype.

At this point in the process, your solution is *still* not going to be perfect—that's the point! Take criticism attentively and use it to gain perspective on your solution. You want to fail *early* so you have greater success later.

FAIL CHEAP—THEN DO IT AGAIN

The feedback obtained by your team will help you design a stronger iteration of your solution. Part of what sets the innovation process apart from traditional program development methods is an acceptance that our solutions are in an ongoing cycle of testing and redesign prototypes. At all stages of the design, we aim to implement in a cost effective manner, but, especially during this stage of development, failing cheap and integrating feedback is critical. Now that you've gathered your first round of information, it's time to integrate it into your concept and redesign your prototype. Interviews and focus groups, whether formal or informal, tend to generate a lot of data. It's up to you to turn those data into insights.

Gather for a redesign meeting to share your feedback and discuss your findings. It's okay if, at the end of this feedback process, your solution ends up looking completely different. You can use a stoplight metaphor to visualize how to move forward. Categorize your feedback under a green light for ideas that received positive remarks and should move forward. Consider how you might build on these ideas to enhance your solution even further. Under the red light, include comments mentioning elements of your solution that must change. Any alarms or red flags identified by the stakeholder you engaged should go in this category. Discuss how to improve these aspects of your solution or what the impact would be if you removed them entirely. What are the lessons you can take from this feedback? Place contradictory comments and feedback the team is uncertain about in the yellow category. Again, decide how these can be modified to give your proposed solution the best chance at succeeding.

Take a critical look at your findings and ask yourselves hard questions. Do the people you interviewed convey confidence in your solution's potential impact? Enthusiasm? Can you address the concerns raised through a redesign of the solution? Do you have to scrap parts of the solution (or even the whole solution) and refer back to the parking lot of ideas generated during the ideation session? How did agency leadership respond to your idea? Did different stakeholders have contradictory views of the proposal? While not every response will have a dramatic impact on your design, even little adjustments will go a long way.

As you continue the innovation process, you will have a chance to modify your solution into one that can be implemented on a small scale and tested. For now, however, keep a big picture view of your innovation. In an ideal context, what would your solution look like? Consider the final solution you would pitch to funders. Why do you believe it would work? What are the elements of it that would make it successful? What kind of resources would be needed? What would it look like in its final stage? Collaboratively construct a vision for your innovation, taking into consideration the insights gleaned from testing your alpha prototype. Your team should build, discuss, and modify the solution until you feel confident investing resources in the next step: beta testing.

DEVELOP YOUR BETA PROTOTYPE

Your beta prototype is the next iteration of your innovation. Here, small-scale, cheap implementation is still the target. As opposed to the alpha prototype, however, here your team is designing a prototype that is small-scale, cheap, *and* functional. Modify your solution to enhance its potential for success and gear the conversation toward the development of a concrete beta prototype that can be tested in the field. If you were to *implement* a first draft of your solution, how would you do it? How you decide to develop the beta prototype will depend greatly on what your proposed solution is.

If the idea is to develop a social enterprise for your homeless shelter, for example, your beta prototype might be to conduct a two-month training program with your residents that culminates in a sale at the end of the test program. Among other things, this will give you insight into what it will take to actually implement the training program, how the participants will respond to the training, who the right population is for you to target, and gauge consumer interest in your final product. If your idea is to develop a social media platform to connect older youth in foster care, you can perhaps start with some basic functionality or build something into your existing social media platforms. While full-scale implementation still requires substantial resources, beta testing allows you to test and modify your solution at a fraction of what it would cost to launch a social enterprise or a new social media platform at full scale.

INterpret your beta prototype as a small, simplified version of your complete solution.
INtertwine existing programs and resources into the development of your beta prototype.
INdicate what success will look like, and be sure to include numbers.
INvite people outside your innovation team to play a role in the review and implementation.

Concretely talking about the resources at your disposal to launch the beta prototype will add an important layer to your discussion. Think of ways you can cut corners in the development yet include all the essential components of your solution. The beta prototype is a smaller roll-out serving fewer people, implementing in fewer sites, including only critical elements. The beta prototype is your second, more developed attempt at creating your innovation. It is still not the final solution, but another step along the way in which you are contributing more resources to the development of the innovation and gathering next-level feedback. Through this step, you can continue to answer questions and gather evidence that will strengthen your ultimate solution. What are the questions you want answered through this beta prototype, and what kind of design will allow you to get those answers? What would be the worst-case scenario during testing? Anticipating constraints will help your team prepare for any kinks that may come up during beta testing. Plan for how you will address these issues that can, and likely will, arise.

Building the Beta Activity

1. Your team is tasked to develop what a small-scale version of your innovation would look like. Open up a brainstorming session by getting into small groups and asking "How might we design a testable version of our innovation that can yield lots of information on the efficiency and effectiveness of the innovation?"

2. Come together as a team and discuss the various ideas generated. Decide which of the testable versions makes the most sense for your team to implement. Consider the following questions:
   • How will this help me understand the reaction stakeholders will have to the solution?
   • Will this help reveal unforeseen challenges, such as staff time, financial resources, interest, and specific issues relevant to the target demographic?
   • How could we measure the success of this beta prototype?
   • Does it incorporate enough of the core elements of our innovation?

3. Design a visual process map (Figure 6.3) to help you identify how your beta prototype will take shape. Think of the activities, time frame, and resources needed for your beta prototype. Use the following questions for guidance:

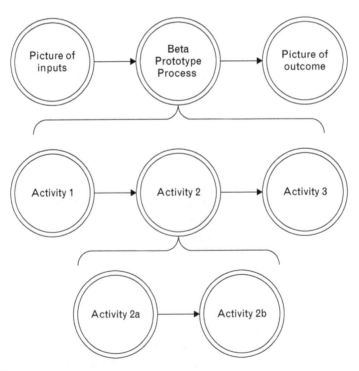

FIGURE 6.3: Process map.

- What mechanisms will you set in place to determine the beta prototype's efficiency and effectiveness?
- What assumptions are you making in the implementation of this prototype?
- How will we check in throughout the course of this implementation?
- How can the activities of the beta prototype complement or conflict with current responsibilities?

4. When the process for your developing beta prototype is determined, decide the responsibilities each team member will assume. Be sure to include any necessary approvals, requests for funding, and specific milestones for your team to check-in.

Your beta prototype will help you identify the best way to allocate time and resources. Use this to answer questions that your alpha prototype was not able to obtain. Be mindful that beta testing will require a significant investment. How will your team make the most out of it? Be practical about the management tools used to launch the beta prototype while continuing to be creative and participatory in your approach.

The beta prototype requires complete commitment from everyone involved. Time and resources have to be dedicated to this testing for it to be successful. In order for you to be ready to launch your beta prototype, your team should be meticulously prepared with all the resources and project planning tools needed to effectively begin any new project. Don't forget—that requires the right energy, too.

TEST, TEST, TEST

The purpose of your beta prototype is to figure out if your idea actually has some traction. Other sectors, like design and engineering, do this quite well. In the nonprofit sector, we can also take advantage of this concept by purposefully implementing elements of our complete idea and evaluating the outcomes. This process will allow you to gauge what's effective, so you can do more of it, and what's not working, so you can fix it.

As with traditional project management, including evaluation measures is an important part of beta prototype planning and implementation. How will your team collect data that will tell you if what you're doing is working? The way in which you collect data will vary depending on your innovation, target audience, and resources. Interviews. Questionnaires. Document reviews. Web analytics. Observations. Use whatever strategies make the most sense for your context, but don't skimp on quality. Evaluating new interventions is important not only to know what is working and what is not working, but to prevent negative unintended consequences that might arise from this new project. Since unintended consequences are by their nature elements you did not prepare for, having evaluation standards will help your team be mindful of identifying and addressing any potential harm to your organization and/or stakeholders. Schedule regular checkpoints with the team to share findings. Checkpoints can also be useful to gather many minds to solve unexpected glitches along the way.

Data will serve two purposes. First, it will give you insight on what you're doing right and what you're doing wrong. This is critical for redesigning your solution in a way that makes the most sense. Cost effectiveness and impact are two key measures to identify. Second, it will give you concrete tools for demonstrating to others that what you're doing has potential. Whether you're targeting funders, people within your organization, or beneficiaries, collected data will inspire confidence where anecdotes fall short. Having various ways to support your claims that your innovation will function as intended will help drive your solution forward.

Whenever possible, triangulate your team's findings. *Triangulation* is a tool that uses multiple data sources to cross-verify your findings. If your data are showing a high impact in one area through surveys, conduct some interviews to help bolster that claim. If qualitative interviews yield positive results, strengthen those findings with administrative data. Getting momentum for your innovation at this point will greatly help its potential for success, and validating research is a useful tool in creating that momentum.

Some important questions to ask yourselves at this point are:

- Is everything going as planned—both with the process of implementation and the expected outcomes?
- What has been successful in our implementation? What has contributed to these successes?
- What have we learned about the resources needed to launch the full idea?
- What has been unexpected about your beta testing?
- Do you need a course correction? What would that look like?
- What steps do we need to take in the short term to move forward?
- Given your initial results, what do you see as the long-term future of your innovation?

Contemplate these questions as you move through your beta testing. Feedback that tells you what's not going well is a good thing! Also consider communication of this feedback and the time dedication needed from the team. While you want commitment from everyone, checkpoints don't have to be exhaustive, but they do have to be regular. A quick team email or a group messaging conversation can do the trick. Beta prototyping is intended as a purposeful space for all these considerations to surface. Pay attention to them instead of looking the other way or sweeping them under the rug. Be confident that asking difficult questions will only help make your innovation (as well as your innovation team) stronger.

DESIGN AND REALIGN

Continuing with the theme of honesty and asking hard questions, have a meeting for the team to come together and discuss how to improve your innovation. Allow a space for everyone to share what they believe worked and what didn't. As not everyone will have information on data collected during beta testing, have people support their arguments with findings whenever possible. Numbers. Quotes. Stories. All are useful in expressing ideas and sharing stories.

Confidence Wheel Activity

1. Place a dot at the center of a large dry erase board or flip chart and draw several line segments radiating from this point. Place tick marks on each segment to create a scale from 0 (the center dot) to 5 (the end of the line). Each line will represent a measure, which your team will use to determine the effectiveness of your prototype.
2. Decide what measures you would like your line segments to represent. Some useful measures include enhances mission, promotes social justice, cost effective, exciting, sustainable, addresses root cause, innovative, level of impact, and inclusivity.
3. Once you have decided what each line segment represents, rank your innovation from 0–5 on each segment and plot it on the line.
4. Connect the dots and discuss the size and roundness of the wheel you have just created. You can decide whether to do it as a team or to do it individually and compare.

Plotting points on a chart will help you visually identify the strengths and shortcomings of your innovation. Use measures that will challenge your prototype to high standards. Think about what is important for your innovation's success. Discuss which of the measures are keeping your circle from being large and round. Also take time to discuss the measure that are ranked high. Are there opportunities to expand those even further? What is your team doing right in these sections that could help inform the others?

How do you rank your confidence in your solution? Assessing the team's confidence on a scale of 1–10 might be a good place to start. While actually ranking may seem difficult, this calls our attention to people's perceptions of potential success. If it's anything below a 6, stop and do some serious thinking about whether it makes sense to continue with this idea. It could be that it's not the right time, and you want to revisit this later. It could be that you need more resources to implement effectively. It could be that your solution just didn't have the impact that you thought it would. That's okay. But, if you're not confident in your solution at this point, investing further resources is not wise. If you're at a 7 or 8, ask yourselves what you need to do to boost your confidence to a 9 or 10. What elements of your solution are you most excited about? Which have the most potential? Take those elements to the next step. Leave what's not working behind and build on what *is* working.

Have an open conversation about how you can modify and enhance your solution. The stoplight metaphor previously used can be applied to this meeting, too. This meeting should be a continuation of ongoing discussions during beta testing. Hopefully, this is the time to speak with concrete information and recommendations for next steps—whether that be full implementation, launching another modified beta prototype, or going back to the drawing board.

As you move further along into having this innovation become a part of the overall agency, give more consideration to how this innovation fits in with the organization's programming as a whole. How can it be better integrated with other programs and initiatives? Even in the innovation's early stages, your team should be purposeful in improving the alignment of the innovation to ensure it clearly complements the work your organization is already doing.

As you consider realignment, pay attention to how you have utilized existing resources within your agency thus far. Think of the existing programs that are already doing complementary work. Are there ways you can build synchronicity between this new initiative and existing resources? How can they collaborate together? Can they share funding streams? Would it make sense for staff from other departments to take the lead in this innovation? Often, other initiatives and connections within an organization can be leveraged to take an innovation to the next level. Use all your resources!

PIVOT, PASS, OR SHOOT

While it might seem like, at this point, you've invested too much to turn back—don't let that fool you. Innovation is a nonlinear process. It might seem logical to go from beta prototype to full implementation, but that's often not the case. Like a basketball player in the middle of the action, you must decide whether it makes more sense for you to pivot, pass, or shoot. For some teams, you might need more time beta testing in order to get more information on your innovation. Other teams might want to overhaul the idea and start again with designing an alpha prototype. It could even be that your innovation is great, but the context at your agency is not ideal at this time to help it thrive.

These are real considerations, and wherever you are at the end of the day is okay as long as your conversation is oriented to designing something with social impact. You want to spend time working on an innovation with potential you believe in, not trying to cover up mistakes or desperately trying to make something work. You're still early on in the game, so this is still a good time to make big changes. Refraining from doing so can have significant repercussions in the future. In innovation, failure and redesign is a natural part of the process.

If you are ready to take the next step toward full implementation, get the green light from agency leadership to move forward. Include them in your major decisions, even if it's simply approving what the innovation team has decided. The more the leadership believes in the innovation and feels they have a say in its direction, the better the chances are of them championing the innovation in the future. In addition to informing the leadership of your organization, update other staff members and stakeholders on your progress and successes. Communicating your work doesn't have to be stale: find creative ways of letting people know what's going on. You can create infographics, make a quick press release, share a video, or post some stats related to your findings on your webpage or around the office. Throughout your entire innovation process, you should be broadcasting your insights to various stakeholders—what better time than now to show off your accomplishments!

After months of long days, ongoing discussions, brainstorming, and data collection, your team has come a long way and has learned a lot. The innovation process is as long as it is rewarding. Regardless of where your team is at this point, pat yourselves on the back. You've just attempted something great.

REFLECTION ON INNOVATING FROM WITHIN

1. The more ideation is practiced, the better a person (and team) becomes. What can you do to promote ideating on a smaller scale?
2. Sometimes ideation sessions don't yield the intended results. What can you do to ensure the best possible outcomes or to encourage the team to try again?
3. Ideation depends largely on establishing the right culture to promote group cohesion, fun, and trust. What worked in your ideation sessions that can be implemented in other parts of your agency?

MAIN POINTS FOR INNOVATING FROM WITHIN

- Expose yourselves to many different types of innovations—social enterprises, mobile tech, interagency partnerships, gamified education—so that you're primed with a variety of possible avenues for solutions during your ideation.
- Ideate big *bold* ideas, using your fieldwork as a foundation for support. When brainstorming, *quantity* is valued over quality.
- Mistakes are welcome at all parts of the innovation process. They help you grow—as long as you approach them honestly and use them as learning opportunities.
- Create, test, learn, and try again. It's an ongoing cycle throughout your innovation process.
- An alpha prototype is a simple model of your innovation that can help you get feedback from stakeholders in a low-resource, cost effective manner.
- When testing your beta prototype, creating various iterations of your solution will help you get meaningful feedback to improve your idea and prove to yourself (and others) that what you're doing works.
- Have regular check-ins with agency leadership and make them feel part of the process. This will especially pay off during implementation.
- The innovation process may appear linear, but it's not! If you have to go back to a previous step in your process, that's okay!
- Move on to full implementation *only* when and if you are firmly confident in your innovation and your ability to drive it forward.

CHAPTER 7

INTEGRATE

C hapter 7 looks into what it takes to not only launch an innovation, but to ensure it's embedded into the organization's culture and work context.

FIGURE 7.1: Integrate model.

Get ready to ...

1. Implement the full vision of your innovation by connecting to resources and assessing impact.
2. Scale the impact of your innovation to reach a broad audience.
3. Connect with other organizations to expand the impact of social innovation in the nonprofit sector.

Congratulations! Only the most promising ideas make it to this stage of the innovation process (see Figure 7.1). By now, your team has likely brainstormed hundreds of ideas to potentially address the issue you're looking at. With those ideas, you have whittled down, discussed, guessed, tested, gone back to the drawing board, and started the whole process over again. Each innovation process is different, but one thing that remains consistent is that the ideas that have made it to the *Integrate* phase are ideas that have been discussed and tested multiple times. They have shown promise that they will address the problem in a new and significant way, and the team is motivated about the potential to drive them forward. Innovations that make it to this point are (among other things) visionary, clever, effective, and exciting.

Feasible: The innovation is something that can be carried out given the current climate and organizational resources.

Sustainable: There are mechanisms and resources in place that will allow the innovation to stand the test of time and weather any financial or environmental hurdles it might face in the future (note that when we talk about sustainability we are focused on all 3 aspects: social, economic, and environmental sustainability).

High social impact: The measured influence of the innovation on your target population is significant and outweighs the associated costs.

To make the leap from beta prototype to full implementation, several rounds of deliberation must have occurred. Through evaluations, team discussions, meetings with your organization's board and leadership, and stakeholder interviews, your team must be confident that this innovation has what it takes to generate sustainable social impact. If you think you are ready to fully integrate your innovation into your nonprofit, stop and ask yourself if the innovation is feasible, sustainable, and will generate high social impact. How do you (and others!) rate your confidence on these measures? Your beta prototyping should have given you greater confidence in answering these questions. By moving forward, you are saying you have already assessed and accepted the risks associated with implementing the full version of your innovation. At this point, you are confident of the impact it will have on the community. You have considered the intended and unintended consequences of your innovation. You have generated enthusiasm and support for your innovation with all stakeholders. You have ensured access to all the necessary resources to help the innovation thrive. You have done a lot of work!

The *Integrate* phase is a commitment to innovation on various levels. One level is that of your innovation. There is a firm belief that the solution has what it takes and that the organization is dedicated to seeing it flourish. Beyond a one-time process, however, *Integrate* is also about using the momentum established during your innovation process to become a more innovative nonprofit. It's about mindfully weaving innovation mechanisms into the structure and culture of your organization. Take advantage of the interest and enthusiasm initiated through this process to grow the innovation work within your organization.

Become an innovation driver. On a broader level, *Integrate* is also about scaling innovation within the nonprofit sector. By sharing findings and resources or forming strategic alliances, we can tap into a world of new possibilities for the nonprofit sector and ideate a bold new vision for the way nonprofits work.

MOVE FROM PROTOTYPE TO FULL IMPLEMENTATION

Innovation can be a test of endurance. It's a long process, one that requires ambition, preparation, and commitment. The last leg of the innovation marathon is to take your innovation from beta testing to full implementation. Most of the ideas generated through the innovation processes never make it to this point—and that's a good thing. If done properly, the innovation process has helped you identify early on those ideas that don't show promise of standing the test of time. Even some of the beta prototypes developed may have failed to meet your team's expectations. At this point in the innovation process, you have come to accept and learn from failures in order to enhance the initial prototypes or scrap them entirely. That's the idea behind prototyping and failing as cheaply as possible. You have seen your idea gradually transition from concept to prototype, which has generated evidence of its promise. By now, though, you have gained enough confidence in your beta prototype to take it to the next level. You're finally ready to implement your full vision for the innovation and broaden its capacity for impact.

Now, it's up to you and your team to ensure you're giving your innovation the best chance for success by mindfully integrating it within your larger organization. By taking advantage of existing resources, human capital, and complementary organizational structures, your team will weave your innovation into the broader agency to promote synchronicity and bolster your innovation's potential.

LISTEN AND ACT

Taking your innovation to the level of full implementation means looking back at your beta prototype, learning from your successes and mistakes, amplifying what works, and ironing out the kinks. The whole process will require some innovative thinking, but it will also rely on traditional project management tools. Prior to investing resources in full implementation, you want to ensure that you have not only asked all the right questions, but that you have also listened carefully and analyzed the feedback you've been given. A prototype that is socially informed through research and feedback will allow you to implement your innovation with greater confidence.

Take a look at the feedback you have gathered. The data should paint a complete picture of your innovation. As a team, compile the information you have gathered and make sense of it by categorizing the data into clusters of complementary information. At this point in your implementation, your team should have a solid understanding of how well your beta prototype performed through the metrics collected. You should have a keen awareness of the reactions from the innovation's users and an overall sense of how it was received. You should know the kind of support you have gathered within your organization and the level of excitement people have around this new idea. And don't forget to assess how the innovation team itself is feeling about the innovation and the process. This can also be a major catalytic factor in the implementation and integration process.

Overheard Activity

1. Have team members individually write down on sticky notes any significant findings from the beta prototyping process that will help inform a full implementation of the innovation. Each observation should be written on its own individual note. This can include outcomes, observations, comments they have heard, acknowledgments, etc.
2. Once everyone has finished, have everyone go around and share their observations with the team. As team members share their observations, cluster them into categories.
3. Discuss the major findings and how to factor them into your team's efforts moving forward. You can use the acronym, *HEAR*, to frame the conversation:
   *H*ope: What potential is there to have social impact?
   *E*vidence: What concrete data was collected?
   *A*pprehension: Are there red flags noted during prototyping?
   *R*esponse: What are internal and external perceptions of the innovation?

The process of analyzing data can be overwhelming depending on the amount of information collected. Finding common themes and clustering findings will help make this process more manageable. Try to maintain an objective perspective on the information shared. It can be difficult to acknowledge when data show a weakness in the innovation, but this is critical for improvement. Conversely, it is equally as important to highlight what's working and to build on those elements to maximize impact.

When looking back at the prototype, be concrete and abstract in your inquiry. Ideally, you would have used both quantitative and qualitative measures to analyze your beta prototype—but there is no need to stop there. Use another layer of interpretation to gain perspective on your implementation. What did your innovation team see, hear, feel, or do during the prototyping that can help inform the impact of your innovation?

Be sure to also consider any critical questions that have been left unanswered. You want to leave minimal chances for surprises as you scale your innovation to its full scope and integrate it within your organization. Confidence in your innovation should be high, and the strengths and gaps should be clear to the team. Note that this doesn't mean that the innovation must be perfect at this point, but only that you have gathered enough information to know the that risk you will take in full implementation is a reasonable one and absolutely worth taking.

Once you have all the necessary feedback to launch the full concept and you're confident about moving forward, it's time to think about the nuts and bolts needed to expand your innovation from beta prototype to full implementation. More than at any other part of the innovation process, traditional project management tools will be helpful here. One of the challenges often encountered at this point is that some teams reflexively make a mental switch from lively, creative innovation sessions to a more traditional, siloed project management atmosphere. Be purposeful about making the implementation tasks as engaging as the other parts of the innovation process and build on the momentum you have initiated to prevent the implementation of your innovation from feeling bureaucratic or overly administrative. An awareness of your team's dynamics and motivators will help you craft the stimulating energy needed to implement your innovation.

During the *Integrate* phase, you should also consider the makeup of your team and whether you have the right personnel needed to launch the full concept of your innovation. The ideators are not always the best implementers. Depending on the size of your agency and the members of your innovation team, you might consider adding people to the team and/or having members of your current team take a less active role. Because you are now looking at a long-term project, the people involved, skills, and time needed will likely shift, and the project might require the integration of new team members. If that is the case, be sure to bring new members up to speed on the innovation's trajectory and on the culture of innovation your team has established.

After testing the beta prototype, your team should have enough insight into those elements of your innovation that are worth expanding upon. It's likely that you've discovered that, in practice, some of the ideas were strong, while others didn't perform quite as expected. For example, if your innovation was to develop a mobile app to educate immigrants about their rights, you have likely learned a few things along the lines of distribution channels, translation, and ease of use. But maybe you also realized that the extra bells and whistles of your app, like offering legal aid, English-as-a-second-language (ESL) opportunities, and a question forum was too much and too confusing for your users. Maybe you realized that the element of the app focused on interacting with law enforcement received the bulk of the attention, and it's worth focusing solely on that particular aspect. To develop your innovation into the best possible solution, you need space and time to mindfully think through the expansion of your innovation and home in on what will be feasible, sustainable, and deliver high social impact.

To fulfill your solution's potential, take a critical and holistic look at your innovation. The Root Down Activity will help your team approach your implementation with consideration for factors that influence the success of your innovation. Among these determinants are factors external to your innovation. You must look outside of the solution itself and see how it fits into the broader work of your agency and the external environment. It could be that your solution is great but that there are organizational or governmental policy shifts that make implementation difficult. Conversely, there can be situations where timing your innovation to coincide with news, events, or policies at the community level can help attract greater support or resources for it. The environmental context of your innovation should be thought of on a broad scale. Factors include and are not limited to economic influences, current events, levels of donation and giving, political interest, other nonprofits and programming, and public perception. Remember that innovation cannot happen in a vacuum; we must strive for inclusivity in the process and purposefully integrate the innovation into the environment in which it exists.

Root Down Activity

1. In this activity, your team will be asked to imagine your innovation as if it were a plant you have nurtured throughout the past several months. To get started, break off into pairs and allow some time for each pair to decide which plant best symbolizes the innovation you have been growing.

2. Next, divide the following questions among the pairs so that each is in charge of answering a few questions. Allow enough time for pairs to come up with responses:

   Weather conditions: What have been some previous storms that have been weathered? Are there any impending weather conditions of which you must be aware?

   Think: What systemic factors influencing your innovation have you had little control over—policy changes, economic conditions, agency turnover, etc.

   Trimming: Sometimes you have to cut branches to help the plant thrive.

   Think: What are some elements of the innovation that might be weighing it down and preventing it from thriving?

   Budding: Where are you starting to see some buds form? What fruits or flowers have started to blossom? Who has stopped to appreciate the flowers?

   Think: What have been intended and unintended consequences of the innovation? What attention has it received from within the organization or community?

   Nurturing and care: What does your plant need to grow? Does your team have the necessary green thumbs? Does your plant need to be transplanted elsewhere?

   Think: Are there other people who need to be integrated into the implementation? What additional expertise is needed to help your innovation thrive?

   Gardening equipment: Are there any new tools needed?

   Think: Are there any tech tools that could help enhance your ability to successfully launch your innovation? What are your general project needs? What financial needs do you have?

   Growing conditions: What are the special considerations specific to this plant?

Think: What are some unique cultural considerations relevant to your target population or social issue that you must keep in mind? How can you further contextualize your innovation to your target population's and/or organization's strategic goals?

Gardening competitions: How does your plant compare to the other plants in the garden? Are there other plants competing for space?

Think: What other innovations or traditional nonprofits are competing in the same market? What sets you apart? How does your innovation better address the issue at hand?

3. Come together as a team and have each pair share its drawings and discussion points.

In the same way that your team has given time, energy, and resources to planting an innovation seed and helping it grow, you are now tasked with strategically implementing the same care and dedication to help the innovation establish roots within your organization. This activity will help you team unearth important considerations by combining the practical with imagination and symbolism. The questions are designed to help your team think broadly about what full implementation will take. Give significant time to understanding how these elements will be leveraged to ensure the sustainability of your innovation. Be sure to encourage creativity and imagery.

For growing the innovation itself, traditional project management tools can help you fully form your solution. Thinking through concrete issues like staffing, budget, timing, and other resources is critical to the success of any solution. The following are a few tools that might be helpful for your team as you grow your innovation. While you are likely familiar with several or most of these tools, they are worth mentioning as they have been shown to be tried and true for developing solutions for nonprofits. As mentioned before, this aspect of innovation can feel bureaucratic to some innovation teams—especially considering the contrast to lively ideation sessions. Put effort into making the implementation process collaborative and engaging.

Tried and True Project Management Tools

Logic models: Useful for identifying the theoretical basis for your solution and connecting it to processes and outcomes. This project management tool can be altered to fit the stage of the innovation, whether it's planning or implementation.

Business model canvas (Osterwalder et al. 2010): This framework provides a broad overview of the implementation process and includes business elements that may be of particular relevance to new, nontraditional innovations in the nonprofit sector.

Gantt charts: A timeline to ensure your innovation stays on task is always handy. The chart can be as simple as you'd like, or you can dress it up to include helpful elements like color coding to assign tasks and responsibilities, milestones and targets, and celebration markers.

Budgets: While this is an obvious component of any project, it must be said that proper budgeting is essential to the development of a successful innovation. Whether you choose to use Excel or other project management software, accurate forecasting will ensure you have money for the lights to stay on. Invite other project managers to help your team think through budgeting needs and areas where in-kind contributions can help offset costs.

Case statements: In a brief, compelling manner, what is the vision of your innovation, and how does that further your mission? A good case statement will make your argument to potential donors in a way that appeals to their logic and emotion.

Pitch deck: Often used with investors, but can also be used to pitch your idea to any number of stakeholders, a pitch deck will give a strong visual and oral overview of your problem, opportunity, solution, and impact.

Thinking about implementation and expansion doesn't have to be an isolated activity for project managers to do behind closed doors. The innovation process is participatory, and the *Integrate* phase is no exception. Co-creating the next steps of your innovation will help you keep workload evenly distributed, continue to integrate values of diversity and inclusion, and maintain the excitement and momentum necessary to carry out ambitious projects. Continue to move around. Continue being deliberate in asking for input. Continue to be visual. Continue to think the (im)possible. And, above all, continue to strive toward sustainable social impact.

Stick 'em Timeline Activity

1. Designate one person to be the scribe for the team.
2. In no particular order, ask people to shout out different activities that have to happen in order to implement your full innovation and have the scribe write each idea on an individual sticky note.
3. Once all the ideas have been shared, go through them as a team and create a visual timeline by arranging the sticky notes in chronological order.
4. After the timeline has been finished, have team members write their names on the sticky notes they will be responsible for carrying out. Some sticky notes will require the efforts of multiple people, and some will only require one person.
5. Take a picture of the timeline and have a team member formalize the end product into a Gantt chart to share with the team.

This activity is a way of creating a Gantt chart in a participatory manner. By making this collaborative, you ensure everyone's opinions are being shared, and you reduce the chance of missing an important part of the implementation process. You can use colored sticky notes to symbolize priorities or assign a specific color to each team member to represent the people leading each task.

As your team advances in the implementation, keep lines of communication open and check-ins regular. Even though the idea of innovation is to fail in the early stages of your prototype, we all know that mistakes still happen, so continue to be attentive to how your innovation is being implemented. If things don't result exactly how they were envisioned or don't go according to your project's timeline, acknowledge what happened and learn from the mistake. As mentioned in the *Initiate* phase—and this is true for the entire innovation process—when we acknowledge failure, we spend more resources learning from and fixing the situation rather than trying to cover it up. That being said, because we are sometimes prone toward the negative, have some fun with it and use the Self-Destruct Button Activity to envision failure in order to prevent it from happening in the first place.

Self-Destruct Button Activity

1. The goal of this activity is to do everything possible to ensure your innovation fails. To help you do so, place a large self-destruct button at the center of your meeting space.
2. Take turns pressing the self-destruct button. Every time the button is pressed, the person pressing it must describe one thing that would cause the self-destruction of your innovation (i.e., don't advertise the event, understaff the program, make the product out of expensive material, etc.).
3. As you describe the destruction of your innovation, have someone visually represent what is happening to your innovation on a dry erase board or flip chart.
4. Go around pressing the button until you have ensured the self-destruction of your innovation.
5. Once finished, discuss the opposite things that need to happen so that the innovation sees success rather than destruction.

Possibly even more helpful than thinking through what is needed for your innovation to succeed is thinking through what is needed to fail. Thinking of the obvious things that will lead to an innovation's failure will bring to light several activities you can put in place to prevent failure from happening.

DROP ANCHOR

Anchor your innovation down into your organization by incorporating as many stakeholders as possible into the expansion of your innovation. Connecting to existing funding streams, aligning with other programs, and clarifying how the success of your innovation is intrinsically tied to the goals of your mission are key areas to address at this stage. Finding commonalities between your solution and other organizational initiatives will ensure that your innovation has longevity within your organization.

One of the many benefits to purposefully including management, board members, and other staff into the innovation process is that synergy between your innovation and existing programs will surface more naturally. Opportunities to promote your innovation or to share internal resources are facilitated when those who manage existing resources already have a stake in your team's innovation and know it well.

Management and board members are also key people who can connect your team with useful resources. Often, they are aware of resources that your team may not be familiar with. Other times, management and board members can provide key links to financial and human resources that may not otherwise be accessible to your team. They may even be privy to events, grants, or policies coming down the pipeline that can be game-changers to your solution. Meetings with management will also help shed light on how to best expand and develop your solution and ensure a common vision for the innovation. The people at this level of the organization have lots of experience implementing new solutions and will be instrumental in asking challenging questions that will help your team anticipate potential barriers. Utilize the human capital of your organization as a unique asset for your innovation. You never know the resources and talent that exists until you invite others along in the process.

During team meetings, ask people for recommendations on implementation, whether it's to discuss implementation issues you've been stuck on or simply to provide feedback and observations. There are many areas throughout the innovation process where you can integrate various stakeholders and make this a truly co-created innovation. You will instill a greater sense of commitment to the solution and cohesion in the implementation in your workplace by bringing more staff members into the conversation. The last thing your team would want is for your solution to fail because there isn't enough buy-in from within your organization or for staff members to feel like this is a completely external initiative that is suddenly being dropped into the workplace. Effective communication with your organization's staff will remind everyone of the work your team has been doing around a specific issue, smooth out potential kinks in your innovation, and help the staff see the value of taking this new direction. Excitement and buy-in are key ingredients necessary for expanding and embedding the innovation within your organization.

Interwoven Activity

1. Identify a list of people, programs, and values that are foundational to your nonprofit. When you have come up with a core list, have the team members select one or a few that they will represent in this activity.
2. Stand in a circle and bring along a ball of yarn. The yarn will represent your innovation. The ball will be passed around between group members. Each time a team member asks for the ball of yarn, he or she will share one way in which the innovation is connected to that person, program, or value of the organization. Each team member should continue to hold onto his or her part of the yarn until the end of the activity—eventually forming a large, interwoven web.

3. When you've exhausted all your responses, interpret the web that has been created. Which people, programs, or values seem to be intrinsically connected with your innovation? How are you leveraging these connections? Which connections seem to be weak or entirely absent? How might this impact your innovation? What can be done about this?

The web will provide a visual representation of how well your nonprofit is integrated into your organization. The more connections there are, the stronger the chance of it persisting within your nonprofit. Use this as an opportunity to make the most out of existing connections and generate continuity where it doesn't already exist.

A common challenge with integrating innovations is that they are perceived as initiatives that are outside the nonprofit itself. Whether it's because they haven't been there since the beginning of the organization, or because they are seen as being started by a subset of the organization, or simply because stakeholders may be uncomfortable with change, it often takes time for people to get on board with a new idea. Anticipate challenges with integration and frame them as opportunities to enhance your innovation's potential. If you predict people will be uncomfortable with a new technology used, be proactive and hold an interactive demo. If your challenge lies in people's skepticism of you innovation, share the evidence you have collected to date and welcome observations and suggestions from outsiders. Invite others into the conversation and be creative in the way you instill your enthusiasm and optimism for your innovation in others. Remember, this is still an innovation with plenty of uncertainties and challenges ahead. Flexibility, openness to criticism, and humility remain key elements!

EVALUATE AND SCALE TO AMPLIFY IMPACT

If you're doing it right, you've been evaluating the success of your innovation all along the way and making any and all necessary adjustments to better target your innovation and its impact. Community work demands that we take a critical look at ourselves and what we're doing to ensure we are acting in a manner that is ethical, influential, and promotes the empowerment of the community. This is true whether you're carrying out the development of a workshop or the implementation of a mobile application. When an innovation manages to capture the attention of a broad public or to stimulate change where there was a significant need, there will be a marked call to expand that innovation. To make this leap, however, evaluation and careful planning are necessary.

EVALUATE SUCCESS

As with any good program, ongoing evaluation is instrumental for confirming that what you're doing is working—and working well. Not only is this general best practice, but it is of particular importance in the innovation space since, most of the time, the methods used and programs developed have not yet established a proven track record. When designing the full implementation of your innovation, you must be sure to include regular checkpoints and feedback loops that will provide the team with data to inform its growth and integration into your organization.

Evaluation metrics in innovation serves two significant functions. One, it allows your organization to have concrete evidence of your program's efficiency and effectiveness. Two, it helps grow the global database of knowledge about the effectiveness of new social interventions and how they impact communities. In order for innovation to persist both within your organization and within the nonprofit sector, evaluation metrics must be routinely collected, analyzed, and shared.

INvest time and resources into evaluating what works—and do more of that! Drop what doesn't work and build on what you're doing right.

INtertwine the activities and resources of your innovation with existing programs and processes within your organization. Share any new assets and/or resources your innovation is bringing in.

INvolve many stakeholders in the implementation and tap into their networks to help you get word (and excitement) out about your innovation.

In innovation, our solutions are never final. We accept that programs, policies, and products must adapt to the context in which they exist. We put systems in place that will allow us to have frequent learning opportunities throughout the implementation process, which can inform modifications to the solution. Therefore, rather than having final versions of our innovations, we instead acknowledge that even our full implementation of the innovation is merely its most recent version.

For us to know how to improve the innovation or to have a good understanding of whether it's being implemented as intended, we must be purposeful about utilizing evaluation metrics. Innovation requires both process and outcome evaluations, with each having more frequent checkpoints than with traditional programs. Because we are dealing with experimental solutions, regular checkpoints will help us take each step in the implementation process with greater confidence, knowing that we are mindfully tracking the way we do things.

When designing your *process* evaluation, ask yourself the following questions:

- Do we have diverse involvement from around the organization?
- How satisfied is our target population with our innovation?
- Are we reaching the target number of people we want to serve?
- Is this innovation inclusive?
- How efficiently are the administrative and staff resources being utilized?
- What is the level of involvement of community stakeholders?
- What are the strengths and limitations of this innovation?
- Are our target outputs and outcomes being met?

When designing your *outcome* evaluation, ask yourself the following questions:

- How has this innovation enhanced our nonprofit's impact on this social issue?
- How are we able to see the social impact within the community?
- Have there been any positive or negative unintended consequences?
- Has this innovation strengthened our relationship with our stakeholders?
- What kind of recognition has the innovation garnered?
- How has this changed our agency's perception of innovation overall?
- How have changes in the external environment impacted our innovation?
- Is this innovation a sustainable solution to the social issue?
- Can and should this be replicated?

Although invaluable, evaluations can also be costly—both in terms of money and time. This doesn't necessarily have to be the case, however. In addition to having periodic evaluations, plan to integrate mechanisms into a feedback loop so that you are regularly receiving cost-effective data on your innovation. You might be collecting ongoing consumer satisfaction surveys, you might be running analytics from a website, you could even be looking at regular attendance records. As with many other parts of the innovation process, how you proceed with implementation will be specific to the unique circumstances to your innovation.

Of course, collecting meaningful data is only one (albeit significant) part of the puzzle. What you do with this information is just as critical. It's important to be open to what the feedback might show and nimble in how you implement any follow-up actions. The data may not always reveal positive things about your innovation. They're not all successful. Innovation is still our best guess as to what has potential—no interventions are certain to work. If you are getting positive results—great! Do more of what works and share your strategies with others within the organization and field. If you are getting results that show weaknesses in your innovation—address them head on. While some innovations show promise in the immediate future, the long-term results may be different, and it's important that we pay attention to the data to prevent any harm that may result from experimental initiatives. Acknowledge the opportunity behind any failure and try again through a more informed perspective. After all, that's why we evaluate, and that's why we innovate.

SCALE YOUR IMPACT

Once your innovation is fully implemented, in full swing, and is securely established within your organization, you might begin to consider scaling your solution. This is an organizational consideration that should be reserved for long after you have launched your innovation and have demonstrated a proven track record. The choice of whether to scale looks different depending on the context of your innovation, but the following five considerations can tell you whether you're at the point to have a conversation about scaling:

1. Are you generating significant, proven impact in your community?
2. Have beneficiaries responded positively to your innovation?
3. Do you have a streamlined process?

4. Is there interest and enthusiasm in expanding your innovation?
5. Is the leadership of your organization in full support of the initiative?

If all five considerations are a go, then think about what it would take to scale your innovation and the implications this would have for your organization and the community. There should be clear processes prior to taking any innovation to scale, so ensure that the process has been clearly defined and that any gaps in services have been addressed. Processes that are too complex will be difficult to replicate and will cause unnecessary issues in communication and implementation. Sometimes, it may be necessary to simplify what's already been done. Take the wisdom and insight you have gathered through your own process and distill it down to its core so that subsequent implementations of your innovation are clear to follow and are free of any unnecessary tangents you may have taken.

Innovations should always be tailored to their environmental context. This is true for brand-new innovations as well as those being scaled. Be sure to incorporate cultural adaptations into your scaling efforts so that any new interventions launched reflect the diversity and nuances of the new communities you will be reaching. Integrate the community's voice by having its members contribute ideas about how to be more inclusive in their context. While certainly not an exhaustive list, your organization should pay careful attention to the following considerations as you contextualize your scaling: community history, gender, sexual orientation, decision-making processes, geography, ability, existing initiatives, and cultural strengths.

Since the *innovation from within* process places an emphasis on teamwork as opposed to an individual leading innovation, scaling the innovation will not depend on an individual genius to move it forward. Often in innovation spaces, scaling can be a challenge without the presence of the individual who pioneered the initial innovation. In this case, however, you are leveraging the power of teamwork and an innovative organization that supports such thinking. As such, scaling initiatives should be met with lower barriers because you won't have to worry about finding one leader to carry the innovation forward. Use this strength of power and knowledge distribution to embolden teams of people to champion scaling efforts.

It's important to consider that scaling can take many different forms depending on both the innovation itself and your organizational context. Consider the following options for scaling your impact:

Expansion: There might be room to grow even beyond your team's initial vision for the innovation. You might develop supplementary programs, additional projects, complementary technology, or other initiatives to expand what you've been doing.

Replication: Why mess with something that's not broken? You might be interested in having your nonprofit essentially launch the same initiative in another site, with some consideration given to modification for cultural and community contexts.

Branching: Let other people in on the action by allowing them to replicate your model. Through branching (developing local branches of a central organization), people from across the country can replicate your innovation by adopting your methodology and implementing it within their own neighborhoods.

Training the trainers: If you're not interested in launching or able to launch another of the same initiatives, you can share your best practices and insight with others through a training-of-trainers model. This will provide others with tools to launch their own similar endeavors.

Dissemination: Even without a formal training or consulting model, you can scale your idea by disseminating your results and practices. Use academic or practice venues to share your experience and results.

Advocacy: You can use various mechanisms to get the word out about your innovation's mission and impact. Consider different ways of promoting awareness, such as tool-kits, dialogues, online media, and policy briefs.

However you choose to grow your impact, be deliberate and methodical about expanding. Spontaneous diffusion of your innovation could cause significant shortcomings in your ability to be proactive in addressing readiness issues. Be sure to be mindful of both internal and external issues affecting potential scaling. Externally, you want to be aware of environmental constraints, including relevant policy, level of donations and giving, and the initiatives of other nonprofits. Internally, consider the timing for your organization, space considerations, scope, pace, interest, and available resources for scaling. Some of the challenges with scaling include that it inherently adds complexity and bureaucracy to your work, not to mention that the process for scaling lacks the creativity of launching the initial innovation. With good foresight, planning, and anticipation, this doesn't have to be the case!

MAKE INNOVATION YOUR COMPETITIVE ADVANTAGE

Once you've completed the marathon that is launching an innovation, keep the momentum going! By this point, you have initiated a culture of innovation within your nonprofit and you have demonstrated that creative, participatory solution-building results in significant benefits to both your organization and the community. Use this to amplify your impact. Think beyond the scope of your individual innovation and also dedicate effort to becoming a nonprofit that innovates regularly. Beyond a one-off project, you have the potential to become an innovative leader in your field. A leader who nimbly responds to what's happening in the community. A leader who is regularly scanning for new opportunities to improve your work, be it through the integration of new technology, development of new partnerships, or the strengthening of existing programs. Become an innovation driver and make innovation your competitive advantage.

Don't let innovation stop with a single innovation project—for that matter, don't let innovation stop with just your organization. *Innovation from within* is concerned with creating intraorganizational impact, but the long-term goal is to advance the nonprofit sector so that it is able to leverage existing resources for the sake of systemic transformation. When you consider going beyond this innovation project, think of the amplification effect that will be possible when you reach out to expand innovation to other nonprofits in your sector through partnerships, information dissemination, resource sharing, or any other mechanisms you can ideate. Different from for-profit organizations, our shared vision as nonprofits gives us the upper hand in establishing broad support networks and collectively creating social good.

Innovation allows organizations to be competitive because flexibility and nimbleness allow fluid movement in times of economic downturn. Creating diversified revenue streams may be one piece of this, but it also means being able to adapt programs and service provision in times of economic austerity. Nonprofits with an innovation mindset are able to retool programs to respond to market shifts and understand when certain programs need to be sunset. Conversely, nonprofits must utilize innovation to leverage times of economic prosperity. Innovation calls us to continually be on the search for new opportunities and to act by leveraging the resources around us.

In addition to financial and programmatic advantage, innovation provides a way to leverage other relationships and opportunities. It can be an important part of a fundraising pitch, attracting new donors or reenergizing the existing donor base. Innovation may support donor stewardship by providing deeper engagement opportunities for those who give. Board members may become more committed because innovation projects offer new ways for them to get involved in the organization. Innovation can strengthen community ties or partnerships by cultivating these relationships as they relate to particular projects.

FORTIFY YOUR FOUNDATION

Establishing a commitment to innovation comes with significant benefits to your organization. If a one-time innovation project can help you create a new idea for how to best utilize new technology, address an emerging social issue your nonprofit is facing, or identify opportunities for generating earned income, imagine what launching multiple innovation projects can do for your organization. By building on the innovation foundation you have just established, you can continue to identify new opportunities for action, leverage existing resources, and anticipate changes in the environment through innovation. Take the momentum you have initiated through your innovation process and utilize it to broaden your innovation work.

The innovation process you and your team just went through was likely full of successes, do-overs, and ah-ha moments. Take a meta-perspective to capture both what these moments were and the factors that facilitated them. What were the dividers and connectors that made your innovation work—or not work? Every iteration of the innovation process provides learning opportunities for your organization to better tailor the process to your context. Take note of how the next innovation process can be conducted with greater success and formalize the process as relevant to your organization. Among other things, consider the time and space for innovation, how your innovation was received inside and outside your organization, motivators for innovation, team commitment, use of available resources, team energy, and the division of labor. What are the elements within the organization that must be present for it to continue to be innovative? Have your team discuss anything and everything that can lead to a more successful innovation process for the next round.

The Ghost of Innovations Yet to Come Activity

1. Break off into three groups—the ghost of innovations past, the ghost of innovation present, and the ghost of innovations yet to come. Each group will imagine themselves as ghosts from either the past, present, or future and will have insight on how innovation processes functioned during their particular era.

2. In these groups, brainstorm all the factors that made innovation possible—or difficult—at the time they were developed and launched. If your group were a ghost visiting the present, what insight would they share? What warnings would they have for you? Think holistically about the dividers and connectors that influenced the success of the innovations. Are the dividers and connectors a result of the innovation itself, or are they a result of the time and context in which the innovation was developed? Take some time to develop your ghost character and think about what each might say regarding the innovation and time he or she lives in.

3. Have each team act out or draw their ghost as if the ghost were visiting the innovation team in the present. What are the major takeaway points you can learn from the three visitors?

This is an opportunity to look, reflect, and project. Reflect on the successes and challenges of your innovation process. What have you learned? Project into the future. What will be necessary to be successful innovators? Each new innovation cycle brings opportunities for enhancing the process. If this is your first time using the innovation process, consider how other new projects have been started and implemented. Be mindful about incorporating how the context in which the innovation was developed affects its outcome. The innovation process should always consider the influence of its environmental context.

Another tool for looking at how to improve your innovation process and capacity is the Innovation Audit Activity used in the *Initiate* phase (Chapter 4). Look back and track the overall progress you have made as an organization. Notice what elements from the audit still require some attention and celebrate the strides you have made as a nonprofit. Acknowledge the people who have helped push your organization to be more innovative and invite people within your organization into a conversation to discuss how being more innovative has impacted their work and the overall mission.

In the *Initiate* phase, we introduced many strategies for introducing innovation and setting an innovation foundation you can build on. It's worthwhile to go back and revisit some of these practices. You might be at a better place to integrate some of these strategies into your nonprofit. At this point, you likely have a better understanding of why some things did or did not work when you first tried implementing them. If it makes sense, try implementing some of these mechanisms again to strengthen the way your organization incorporates innovation practice into the workplace.

Take additional steps beyond the foundational building blocks for your nonprofit to truly embrace innovation. What you do depends on the success of previous attempts, available resources, and a number of organizational factors. Consider the following strategies for enhancing *innovation from within*:

Commit to an innovation budget: Surely by now you understand that innovating without a budget is very difficult. Allocating specific funding to innovation is a significant practice that demonstrates both practical and symbolic support for innovation—even a small innovation fund can have a substantial impact.

Ideate regularly: Just as you might hold weekly meetings, make brainstorming a regular event. Create meetings or events to come together as an organization and identify new opportunities for action. Make sure you have developed clear mechanisms for stakeholders to develop and share new ideas.

Offer trainings: Trainings help staff develop new skills and keep existing skills sharp. In innovation, we value different ways of thinking and different ways of viewing opportunities. When we offer trainings, we add new tools to our staff's tool belts, tools that can directly and indirectly lead to more innovative thinking.

Institute rewards systems for innovation: People appreciate being appreciated. Rewards for innovation don't have to be monetary. They can also include bonus time off, formal recognition, or mentorship opportunities. There are infinite ways of showing staff that their innovative thinking is valued.

Design physical and cultural spaces that promote innovation: Your environment influences your actions. Design spaces to be stimulating, promote exchange and dialogue, and make people feel inspired. In addition to an energizing physical space, institute routines that instill a culture of innovation in the workplace.

Include innovation in your mission and vision statements: If innovation is truly at the core of what you do and who you are, express it to the world. Tell others that innovation is important to you and why it's important—what more significant way to do that than your mission and vision statements?

Develop an innovation council: Those who have launched innovations within your organization have gleaned lots of expertise in innovation. Utilize their knowledge and connect them into the ongoing innovation work. Invite those who have already participated in innovation cycles to be a part of an innovation council that can help provide mentorship to current innovation projects.

Use the innovation process to regularly assess for new areas in which to take action. Scan the outside environment to identify potential obstacles or opportunities. Inspiration can come from the development of new technology, significant political shifts, local events being sponsored, or new funding streams. Events happening outside your organization can have a profound impact on your work. Just as they can cause setbacks in your work, external factors can also help spark new resources and opportunities for your nonprofit. Continual assessment and inspiration should guide the innovation process to be ongoing and continual, not to stop with just one success.

Just as innovation requires purposeful commitment and strategies, it also requires a mind-shift that allows these changes to emerge. We only invest in that which we value. In this vein, innovation must be viewed not as something extra, not as something to be done when everything else is complete. It is not something to be viewed as a burden. Rather, innovation is a competitive advantage. Innovative organizations can respond to new challenges, changing resources, and new populations of need. They can nimbly shift organizational resources and priorities to keep up with social, economic, and environmental shifts. Innovation allows an agency doing its work to be able to respond to new challenges in an effective way. With advances in medicine, longevity, changes in the environment, climate issues, and globalization, we will no doubt see shifts in social problems and the emergence of new challenges. Organizations that are innovation drivers and have embedded innovation strategies are able to meet these demands and respond swiftly.

Organizations can also leverage their innovation skillset toward other advantages. For example, if through innovation you strengthen community connections, you can use those connections in other capacities. If you strengthen technology skills, you can you use that to enhance operations. Innovation skills that build leadership and promote team building can have multiplicative effects on the organization's human capital. The innovation process may broaden skills around assessment, research, and intervention design. Using these skills, resources, and assets to support other work has a cross-fertilization effect that supports organizational capacity.

As an innovation driver, you are prepared to . . .

- Use innovation to strengthen board member engagement, staff retention, and consumer participation.
- Support financial fluidity during times of economic scarcity.
- Use flexibility and nimbleness to retool or sunset programs that are no longer viable.
- Garner all available resources and tools to respond to emergent social problems.
- Exploit new opportunities to serve populations of interest in more effective, more efficient ways.
- Cultivate donor relationships through the opportunity and appeal of innovation.
- Leverage gains made in personnel or skill development related to innovation projects to support organizational capacity.

GO VIRAL

If we really want to impact social change on a broad level, innovation must reach beyond your individual nonprofit. There are multiple pathways for making this a reality. A first logical step is to make the impact of your innovation known to other nonprofits and collaborators. Make information accessible between each other and share what's worked and what hasn't. You can share the value of integrating innovation processes with other nonprofits and help them navigate any challenges that you encountered throughout your own experience. Expanding innovation throughout the sector will result in stronger network of support for our community because weaving our collective efforts can help streamline processes and enhance our services. As nonprofits, we have the benefit of sharing a common social goal—let's take advantage of that and strengthen our chances of generating social change through collaboration and resource sharing.

When you establish strategic alliances with other organizations, you can truly expand the reach of your nonprofit. These alliances can take on many forms depending on the level of commitment and resources. One small strategy for generating large impact is to do your part in making innovation evidenced-based—and sharing it. If you've been tracking the results of your innovation, by now you know what works and what doesn't work. The short-term outputs and long-term outcomes of your innovation can be incredibly helpful in giving validity to new interventions. Tracking and sharing the results of your innovation work will add validity to the use of innovation in the nonprofit sector and will generate an argument for supporting new ways of addressing old problems. Whether it's through the development of an interorganizational innovation database or simply by generating reports for funders and stakeholders, do your part in diffusing the impact of innovation.

Another way to amplify your impact is to share the results of your innovation work with peer organizations. If you've implemented a promising program, other nonprofits might be able to implement elements of your program by tailoring it to their circumstances. They might be able to reach new consumers interested in engaging with your innovation. Or they might be able to benefit from some of the data you've collected during the *Investigate* and *Integrate* phases. Any ah-ha moments that you had throughout your innovation process are likely to also be useful to other nonprofits targeting the same or similar issues.

In innovation, we know that things don't often happen as they are intended. We are subsequently confronted with two different results: intended and unintended consequences. This is another area that is useful to track and share. Though they can sometimes be positive and sometimes be negative, unintended consequences are useful learning experiences that provide a perspective that was previously hidden from view. Observe, analyze, and anticipate what these consequences can mean for your organization and the sector. Sharing learning experiences with other nonprofits is a way to help each other navigate difficult times and to acknowledge the challenges we face in the social sector when balancing social impact and experimental initiatives. Openness to this reality will help nonprofits embrace the struggles of failing and celebrate the triumphs of boldly innovating.

Other nonprofits are just one of many key stakeholders you should consider when thinking about disseminating information. Think about the learning experiences you have had throughout your innovation process and consider what additional stakeholders could benefit from this information. Could it be people who participated in your focus groups? Could it be policy-makers? Could it be current or potential funders? There is likely to be a long list of people who should know about the insights you've acquired while innovating. Invite people from within your organization to discuss what information would be useful to share and whom it should be shared with. Don't stop there, however. Brainstorm the various mechanisms available for you to disseminate this information. How can you best share your insight with these stakeholders? Is it by participating in a town hall meeting? Using social media to present quick facts? Arranging an interview with your local TV station? Presenting your results at a conference? Be creative in how you will make the fruits of your labor known, and celebrate your efforts to make social innovation go viral.

REFLECTION ON INTEGRATING FROM WITHIN

1. What were the most significant barriers your team faced throughout the integration process? What should be done next time you go through the innovation process to ensure a different outcome?
2. Why is it important for you and your nonprofit to be an innovation driver? How can you remind yourself and others of this?
3. Reflect on your innovation process up to this point. What are the aspects you are most proud of? How can you celebrate this success?

MAIN POINTS FOR INTEGRATING FROM WITHIN

- Analyze the information collected during beta testing and determine how it can inform your full implementation. Consider what worked, what didn't work, and what resources were critical for success.
- Use traditional project management skills, but be sure to continue to be fun, visual, and participatory in your approach.
- Invite board members, management, and other staff to discuss implementation as they might have access to resources and information that can help your innovation thrive. Bring in any new team members who might be needed during the implementation phase. The innovators are not always the implementors.
- Intertwine your innovation with what's happening in other areas of your nonprofit. Share resources to promote synchronicity and enhance the chance that your innovation will stand the test of time.
- Formalize your innovation process. Identify the learning experiences you have had throughout this innovation process and document them to help inform the next round of innovation.
- Make a larger commitment to embracing innovation by implementing some of the following organizational strategies: commit to a budget, ideate regularly, offer trainings, institute rewards systems for innovation, design physical and cultural spaces that promote innovation, include innovation in your mission and vision statements, and develop an innovation council.
- Claim an identity as an innovation driver and affirm new innovation skillsets as part of your competitive advantage. This will help your organization integrate for community empowerment, increase staff retention, and be more nimble in times of economic hardship.
- Share the insights you have had throughout your innovation process with a variety of stakeholders both inside and outside the organization. By creating a network of innovative nonprofits, you can amplify the impact of your organization's work.

PART III

INNOVATION
FOR THE FUTURE

Through this book, you have considered an expanded definition of social innovation and multiple pathways to achieving innovation. You have reflected on the strengths and challenges for nonprofits engaging in this work and studied a structured process for engaging in innovation. You have worked at the individual level in Part I redefining innovation and its relationship to the nonprofit sector. You have unpacked the Nonprofit Innovation Model in Part II, supporting innovation within organizations, and been engaged with activities and strategies for application. Perhaps you and your team have successfully completed an innovation project. The book has challenged you to take the content and work to unleash innovation within your organization. But if the book stopped there, then it would only partially achieve its mission. *Innovation from within* is certainly about retooling and reenergizing nonprofit leaders for their own agency work, but it is also a call to action for the sector. *Innovation from within* is designed to stimulate a broader conversation; to stimulate dialogue across organizations to begin to imagine and shape a new nonprofit sector—one that generates new solutions and leads the social innovation field. Through this work, there is the possibility to champion a sector that shares a vision for ameliorating social problems through new initiatives, creativity, and collaboration. Now, the goal is to look beyond the work of each individual organization and toward a future where nonprofits as a whole are engaged in innovation.

In chapter 8, you will be challenged to think about the future of nonprofits. Nonprofits leaders need to engage in broader dialogue around social innovation and further define concepts that are relevant to the sector. This work includes developing definitions that acknowledge and support intrapreneurship and the benefits existing organizations bring to innovation. Nonprofits should consider what resources need to be deployed to develop and sustain new initiatives. Beyond structural and financial resources, innovation requires the development of human capital. This requires new training and activation of a leadership pipeline oriented towards innovation.

Chapter 9, Build the New Nonprofit DNA, includes a call from the authors for nonprofit leaders to deeply embed innovation in the nonprofit sector and begin to claim innovation as a critical goal for nonprofits. Now we are arguing that innovation is presented not merely as just an option, but as a necessity for the sector. Through this approach—this change to the nonprofit DNA—organizations can amplify impact and create lasting social change.

Part III provides the blueprint for how to move from the individual reflective work of Part I where you learned social innovation concepts and the organization level work in Part II engaging with the Nonprofit Innovation Model, to sector level change. Building on early foundations, Part III provides strategies to help create a nonprofit sector where innovation is a core value and a core competency.

ENVISION THE FUTURE OF NONPROFITS

Chapter 8 prepares you to think beyond the organization and prepare the nonprofit sector for engagement in innovation work.

Get ready to ...

1. Use social innovation concepts and research to challenge traditional nonprofit paradigms.
2. Mobilize new resources to support innovation.
3. Activate the next generation of social innovation leaders.

Developing a nonprofit sector that is ready and willing to take on innovation as a core value requires a vision for what that entails, but also structures and supports to make it possible. While Part I has prepared you with the core definitions of social innovation and deepened your belief about the value of innovation for existing agencies, and Part II has provided structures for your organization to engage in innovation work, Part III is about moving beyond individual and organization, towards the sector. To do that requires that social innovation is defined and conceptualized in a way that includes nonprofit work. Social innovation can be deeply embedded into agency work and challenge traditional views of the sector. Innovation demands the development and acquisition of new resources, and the mobilization of new talent. The goal of this chapter is to provide the framework for guiding that broader work.

RESEARCH AND REDEFINE: NONPROFITS AS THOUGHT LEADERS IN INNOVATION

As Chapter 2 elicited, nonprofits have a lot to add to the field of innovation. The work has the potential to transform responses to social problems and create sustainable, scalable solutions. In order for that to happen, the nonprofit sector needs to claim its role and its commitment to innovation for social impact. The sector needs to value its contributions to the field and encourage private and public agencies to recognize that role. Leaders from nonprofit fields, like nonprofit management, social work, and human services, must stand beside those from business, design, engineering, and computer science to drive the innovation conversation.

Driving that dialogue is about creating new definitions and conceptualizations for social innovation that embed strategies and approaches to innovation specific to nonprofits. Current concepts do not take an organizational perspective into account. Further, conceptualization of social innovation has not been adjusted to align with the facilitators or challenges of innovation in the nonprofit context. Additionally, social innovation concepts are quite distinct from the organizational change literature. Nonprofit innovation paradigms are about broad adoption of new technological, administrative, process, or product innovations (Damanpour 1991) but are not directly about response to social issues. A new social innovation paradigm should embed nonprofit approaches in both process and outcome.

To do this requires both conceptual thinking and research. Building the evidence base for social innovation underscores that these paradigms work in practice. Research supports an understanding of barriers and facilitators to innovation, allowing agencies to learn from the experiences of others. Moving beyond case-based and anecdotal evidence supports a deeper understanding of how social innovation works in particular circumstances. The field as a whole must begin to engage in and support this type of research.

Attention to current knowledge-building around implementation science and dissemination uptake helps support this goal of rethinking social innovation. While these fields are about moving evidence-based interventions into practice settings, research in the social innovation arena can learn from these approaches.

The field of dissemination relates to the distribution of information related to a particular practice and the eventual uptake or use of the practice. In this field, strategies like systematic reviews that bring together multiple research findings and the use of opinion leaders to spread practice have shown mixed success with dissemination (Waddell 2001). Strategies that simultaneously engage the academic audience with the practice community create better opportunities for dissemination and use. Collaborative models of practice and research show promise for dissemination and implementation. Funding mechanisms that support this type of collaboration and dissemination in general show potential. In the area of social innovation, the focus on collaboration seems critical for fieldwide acceptance of innovation strategies. Furthermore, creating linkages between academic institutions and the practice community could bolster the potential for impact. Research needs to examine dissemination strategies and support cross-agency learning.

In the related field of implementation science, implementation drivers provide some insight into how to move efforts from being organization-specific to addressing problems for the field. Implementation drivers are thought to support greater uptake and sustainability of interventions (Fixsen, Blase, Naoom, & Duda 2013). Competency drivers are mechanisms that support one's ability for implementation, organizational drivers are mechanisms that create organizations that are hospitable to new interventions, and leadership drivers are specific leadership strategies that create the right environment for implementation. Borrowing from this research suggests the need for the right staff recruitment, training, coaching, and evaluation to drive competency. At the organizational level, it requires decision-support data systems, supportive administrative supports, and external systems interventions to create the right resources for success. For leadership that drives implementation, there is a need for both technical leadership and adaptive leadership (which involves aligning practice to mission, building consensus, and providing clear feedback channels). Borrowing from these concepts suggests that social innovation research should examine how to build a field with the competencies, organizational structures, and leadership to support such innovations.

A sector that galvanizes new social innovation thinking . . .

- Supports the development of new definitions and conceptualizations of social innovation that include nonprofit perspectives.
- Engages in new research efforts on social innovation in the nonprofit sector to inform cross-agency dialogue and advance the knowledge base.
- Builds collaborative networks with practitioners and academics to create research around innovation and improve the likelihood of adoption.
- Borrows concepts from dissemination and implementation science to enhance social innovation thinking.

ADVOCATE FOR TOMORROW: DEVELOP THE SECTOR'S RESOURCES FOR INNOVATION

The challenge of innovation is not simply doing one innovation project, but rather it is translating the one to many and creating a sector with the resources to continually innovate. Paul Light (2008) reminds us,

> Heroes wear out and fear cannot be a motivator for long, especially in the absence of the participation, autonomy, and shared goals that we find in most innovative organizations. Thus the much greater challenge is to produce socially entrepreneurial activity twice, thrice, and more—that is, to create socially entrepreneurial activity as a natural act. (p. 20)

It is this doing of innovation over and over that becomes the challenge for the sector. In the for-profit sector, we see the ability to constantly and nimbly adapt as a core organizational strength with tremendous financial payoff. In nonprofits, we are challenged to make innovation an organizational priority and to find the resources for investment. Resources and competing demands make the potential for ongoing innovation more daunting.

To engage in innovation in this continual and repetitive way necessitates a change in priorities and resource alignment. Dan Palotta is eloquent in his calls for nonprofits to invest more in overhead and risk-taking, to have time for experimentation, and to invest in solving problems at scale (Pallotta 2013). This is the type of reinvestment and rethinking that is needed to start engaging in innovation on a regular basis. It requires greater investment and attention to make innovation happen. And, like a muscle, the more it is practiced, the easier it becomes.

Working with funders and private donors, we must engage in conversations that make investment in innovation a priority. We need to develop funding sources that allow for experimentation and failure rather than investing only in scaling or service provision. The sector needs to develop funding sources that acknowledge and celebrate intrapreneurial activity rather than favor investment in new organizations. Building the resource base for innovation may require new funding streams and realignment with foundations.

Nonprofits also need to get serious about market-based strategies and how they may support work. Earned income strategies may not be a magic bullet, but, in some cases, they may support other work, supplement existing programs, or play a role in employing or supporting program beneficiaries. The nonprofit sector has a clear mission of alleviating social challenges—the focus should be on using all available means to achieve this, whether they involve profit or not.

A sector with resources for innovation . . .

- Works with foundations, government, and private donors to create realistic expectations around overhead, spending needs, and resources that support innovation.
- Develops funding sources that allow for experimentation and risk.
- Understands that diverse funding sources may be required to commit to traditional service provision and innovation.
- Engages in real conversation about failure and what we can learn.
- Considers the potential of earned-income or market-based strategies.

NEXT GENERATION LEADERSHIP: PARADIGMS AND SKILLS FOR THE FUTURE

The power of *innovation from within* is one that has the potential to change an organization's work and invigorate new ways of generating social change. But to elicit change that goes beyond one organization means developing a sector with the skills, resources, and willingness to engage in innovation work. As Tushman and Nadler reminded us in 1986,

> There is nothing mysterious about innovation: it doesn't just happen. Rather it is the calculated outcome of strategic management and visionary leadership that provide the people, structures, values, and learning opportunities to make it an organizational way life.

The nonprofit sector needs to build the pipeline of leadership that can manage this task.

Nonprofit management, social work, public administration, and human service programs need to be realigned to purposefully develop leaders who can nimbly operate in this new environment. The inclusion of core management skills (e.g., finance, budgeting, human resource management, strategy) and core nonprofit skills (e.g., grant writing, assessment, project management, and fundraising) may no longer be enough. Programs need to consider how to integrate content on social innovation, social entrepreneurship, social intrapreneurship, and social enterprise. They can look to include content on design thinking, innovation cycles, social impact assessment, and social impact bonds. Enhanced pedagogy that includes labs, case studies, innovation competitions, consulting efforts, and technology may support teaching these new skills.

In *Leaders Make the Future*, Bob Johansen (2009) outlines 10 specific skills for leaders of tomorrow. He focuses on the *maker instinct*, which is the ability to build and grow while connecting with others in the process. He identifies core skills, including rapid prototyping, dilemma flipping (redefining complex challenges and threats as opportunities), and commons creating (nurturing shared assets), as skills that are endemic to innovation work. In a world of volatility, uncertainty, complexity, and ambiguity (VUCA), it is leaders with this innovation skillset who will emerge to successfully guide for social impact. New teaching paradigms are needed to train nonprofit leaders of tomorrow with this emergent skillset. Creating a nonprofit pipeline with innovation as a core competency prepares the sector.

A sector with emergent leaders for innovation . . .

- Communicates the value of innovation in training and preparation for nonprofit work.
- Considers traditional and nontraditional skills for emerging leaders.
- Realigns professional education in related fields (nonprofit management, social work, public administration, and human services) with the demands of an innovative sector.
- Purposefully develops a new nonprofit leadership pipeline that embeds innovation and skills for the future.

REFLECTION FOR ENVISIONING THE FUTURE OF NONPROFITS

1. What concepts of social innovation are inclusive of the nonprofit sector? What are exclusive of the sector? In Part I, you were asked to reflect on your own definition of social innovation. Do this again and consider whether your definition has expanded.
2. Examine a particular area or issue you are passionate about and consider how that work is funded. Are there sources for experimentation and prototyping?

Consider one solution to the issue and generate an expansive list of potential ways to fund it.

3. Reflect on your own training and preparation. How have you been adequately prepared for innovation work? What other preparation would you have needed/ or liked to receive? How might you (or your organization) consider training and leadership development that supports innovation work?

MAIN POINTS FOR ENVISIONING THE FUTURE OF NONPROFITS

- Nonprofits need to be engaged in dialogue and conversation about innovation. Working with leaders from business, design, engineering, policy, and computer science, nonprofit leaders need to support definitions of social innovation.
- Current social innovation paradigms are often exclusive or less forthright in their inclusion of existing organization. Concepts of innovation should be developed that incorporate these perspectives.
- Social innovation needs research to build the evidence base and inform interdisciplinary approaches to the field.
- Innovation takes resources. The sector can work with funders, including foundations, government, and private donors to create expectations around what is required to do this work and what is needed to allow for experimentation.
- Consider diverse funding sources, including earned income and market-based strategies.
- Supporting innovation requires investment in human capital. This means rethinking training for emergent leaders and developing professional education that aligns with these goals. For social innovation to be sustainable requires a leadership pipeline that is committed and has the capacity to develop, implement, and sustain innovation.

BUILD THE NEW NONPROFIT DNA

Chapter 9 challenges the nonprofit community to rethink its role in innovation.

> **Get ready to ...**
>
> 1. Claim the role of nonprofits within innovation space.
> 2. Reimagine the potential of the nonprofit sector.
> 3. Amplify social impact through *innovation from within.*

As innovation is more broadly adopted by individual organizations, this book hopes to stimulate new discussion around the potential for innovation to reshape the nonprofit sector. The new nonprofit sector is one where innovation becomes the new norm and is considered a competitive advantage to a nonprofit agency. As innovation becomes more deeply embedded in nonprofit organizations, the sector amplifies its impact on problem-solving.

Innovation has the potential to become not just a critical part of nonprofit organizations, but also the place for other sectors to test ideas. In our recent work with nonprofit organizations around innovation, there was the shared sentiment that nonprofit agencies have been and can continue to be the testing ground or incubator for solutions to social problems (Pitt-Catsouphes, de Zengotita, & Berzin 2013):

> I would argue that the nonprofit sector is inherently an innovative sector . . . .. We prototype programs, ideas, and solutions. (McLaughlin Associates, as quoted in Pitt-Catsouphes et al. 2013)

Even beyond testing social solutions, the for-profit sector could begin to leverage nonprofit experience around community engagement, assessment, and diversity. Innovation can create new relationships with government, with nonprofit organizations acting as the drivers who test new ideas. The social impact bond model that pairs nonprofit organizations as innovators with private investors and the government is one such example. Nonprofits have the potential to implement the pilot in citywide or even national initiatives.

The new nonprofit not only has core competencies around innovation, but is also nimble and quick enough to be able to respond to change as needed. With social problems rapidly changing and crises coming more frequently, nonprofits need the ability to respond in the moment. Changing our approaches to be responsive to these demands is critical.

To create this new nonprofit DNA requires shifts in investors and/or funder relationships. It suggests new funding models that support experimentation and innovation, a new funding climate that rewards innovation and social impact. This new funding climate would also reflect an acknowledgment of the critical role of overhead in supporting nonprofit sustainability and impact. The expectation of being successful with funding constraints that prevent securing the best talent, limit budgets on marketing and advertising, and impede the use of commercial strategies leaves nonprofits unlikely to continue to grow and produce impact (Pallotta 2008). The same is true for innovation. If we expect the sector to innovate and continue to produce better, more effective, more efficient results to some of the world's most challenging problems, we need a funding structure that supports investment in innovation and experimentation.

The new nonprofit DNA is about creating a climate where nonprofits not only can be innovative, but also are expected and resourced to be innovative. Social innovation is about developing transformational responses to social problems, and nonprofits need to be at the center of its emergence. Visible social innovation leadership has come primarily from the fields of business, public policy, engineering, and design. While new approaches to social problems benefit from broad contributions across disciplines, nonprofits have the opportunity to play a critical role in directing the next generation of social innovation. Nonprofits represent the bulk of organizational resources put toward solving social problems and bring competencies that are critical to thinking in this area. Nonprofit leaders' expertise in assessment, strengths-based or community-led practice, and ethics provide important contributions to social innovation.

There is almost universal agreement that social innovation is about solving complex social issues that impact communities. Too often, however, the laser focus on solution generation means that the complexity of these issues is overlooked. Nonprofits place particular emphasis on the importance of social justice, assessment, understanding root causes, and identifying possible unintended consequence. Leveraging this expertise means deeper, more responsive solutions to difficult problems.

While many professions recognize the importance of "customer-led or client-led" innovation initiatives, nonprofit practices leverage participant direction and empowerment not only as a means to the end of innovation, but also as being essential to the sustainability of the innovation. Nonprofit practitioners have long-standing experience in developing and implementing social service programs and in working in concert with community. When this is appropriately leveraged, this experiential capital could be an asset for both launching and sustaining social innovation efforts.

And perhaps most important to this discussion is that existing organizations bring instant and automatic scale and sustainability to the solving of social problems. Nonprofits have developed structures, organizational assets, and existing scale. Leveraging these assets changes the social innovation dialogue from one about entrepreneurship and scaling to one about improvement and transformation.

Beyond the sustainability of innovation programs and policies, nonprofits have a demonstrated commitment to shrinking and eradicating social problems. This ethical commitment, proven leadership, and distinct competency base form the underpinnings of a new nonprofit DNA that draws on the past with a recognition of the need for new approaches that harness every available tool for impact.

As one nonprofit leader recently told us, "In the midst of changing and turbulent times, innovation helps us consider how we can best fulfill our mission, what we should do today, and how that differs from what we should do tomorrow" (Pitt-Catsouphes et al. 2013). The new nonprofit DNA creates organizations and a sector that fulfills that mission. *Innovation from within* is not just about stimulating change from within your own organization, but also about transforming the way we solve systemic issues within the sector and use innovation to create a bold, new future.

REFLECTION FOR BUILDING THE NEW NONPROFIT DNA

1. Nonprofits have considerable expertise around community engagement, assessment, and diversity. How might each of these be used to support innovation efforts?
2. Consider a recent social innovation effort. Reflect on how values of social justice, community engagement, and empowerment are embedded (or not) in the effort. What could be done to insure that community, justice, and empowerment are front and center?
3. Imagine a nonprofit built for innovation—What would it look like? What resources would it have? How would its leaders be trained? Consider broadly everything that would be embedded in this dream organization.

MAIN POINTS FOR BUILDING THE NEW NONPROFIT DNA

- Nonprofits of the future will embed innovation as a core practice and core value.
- New nonprofits not only embed innovation thinking into their work, but bring core competencies around community engagement, assessment, and diversity to the field of innovation.
- As nonprofits provide the bulk of the response to societal problems, their visible leadership is critical for social innovation.
- Nonprofits must include values around social justice, community engagement, and empowerment in social innovation efforts.

- Nonprofits (often) have scale, demonstrated sustainability, and organizational assets—these are paramount to the ability to develop, implement, and sustain innovation that responds to social issues.

CONCLUSION

Innovation from within calls for a transformation—transforming you, transforming your organization, and transforming the nonprofit sector so that we are proactively utilizing all of our existing resources to create the sustainable social change in our communities we know is possible. Beginning with you, the individual, it's about creating a paradigm shift to acquire and integrate innovative ways of thinking that reshape the way we engage social problems and their solutions. It's about going the extra mile and proposing what a nonprofit could look like if it has an entire group of dedicated collaborators with new, innovative resources for driving social change. It's about dreaming of a future where we as a sector are committed to networking, building new evidence-based practices, and forging paths for the radical justice work that is needed today.

The social sector has been changing to include a diverse set of actors working to address a wide array of persistent and new social issues. As nonprofits, it's imperative that we not only keep up with the dialogue, but that we play an active role in promoting social justice through all available avenues. We have a distinctive perspective on the way we frame and understand social problems. This, along with other strengths within nonprofits such as our human capital, community relationships, and existing funding streams, make it fundamental that we engage in the social innovation work being done.

Social innovation is an opportunity to leverage new resources, retool our work, and refine our organizations to better address social problems. Yes, we have previously innovated in the sector through various initiatives, but now we have the opportunity to branch out and do things with new tools and new processes. Technology provides a space for us to engage stakeholders at a whole new level, whether they are next door or across the world. Design thinking opens our minds and unleashes our creativity to examine and address social issues through the perspective of a beginner and with deep empathy for the user. Social enterprises break traditional funding mechanisms and provide a platform for economic sustainability within nonprofits. These and other opportunities are what we must leverage to create the spaces we want for our communities.

The trajectory of this book aims to take you far. In Part I, we made an appeal to use an intrapreneurship perspective to reinvent oneself and the organization. Rather than starting something from zero, to utilize the richness that already exists within the nonprofit context to build new partnerships, establish a distinct work culture, create new programs or influence public policy. Beginning with the way we conceptualize social innovation and how it fits in the context of nonprofit work, the first challenge is to ready yourself for thinking like a game-changer. Speaking the buzzwords, learning through examples, integrating new concepts, and reflecting on what this all means for you and the social change you strive for. We also looked at what these concepts might look like within an innovative nonprofit. What does it mean to have a work culture that not only tolerates, but celebrates failure? What are the right conditions to promote innovation within nonprofits? Who are the people that I need on my side? All of this to set the stage for you and your organization to build your own social innovation initiatives.

The path of a lone entrepreneur can be solitary, so in Part II we encouraged you to build a team of like-minded supporters. Now that you've discovered what it means for a non-profit to be innovative, in Part II you acquired the tangible tools needed to make it a reality. Taking the concepts from Part I and bringing them down to a practical level, Part II provided step-by-step companionship on the innovation journey, using the Nonprofit IN Model. While not always linear, the innovation process is a guide for stimulating an organization that establishes innovation within its work culture and within its programming. The IN Model is intended to be an iterative process that allows for innovation to occur not just once with a single project or product—but as a continual process that becomes a part of the organization.

Meetings, games, observations, activities, planning, and analyzing were only some of the key ingredients that made Part II rigorous and light-hearted. The innovation process was an opportunity for you and your team to engage with social issues through different lenses and with a different mindset. The process of imagining, trying, failing, and trying again, equipped you and your team with field strategies for promoting social change by combining elements from various sectors, including design, business, drama, tech, and social work to make your solutions robust, multi-faceted, engaging, and sustainable.

Going the extra mile, Part III put forth an invitation to transform your organization into a nonprofit that can not only launch an innovation, but can lead social sector change. Recognizing the need for broad action, we must not remain at the level of the individual intrapreneur or the individual project or the individual nonprofit—we must seek to amplify the potential impact of social innovation and reach a broader audience. Through nonprofit networks, integration of new technology and by forming new professionals with diverse skillsets, we aim to build a sector that embraces innovation and the opportunities it opens. Part III reenergizes our thinking and our work, not as an individual, not as an organization, but as a sector that has the potential to reshape the way we respond to social issues.

Innovation is meant to inspire. It stimulates curiosity and pushes you to wonder 'what if.' *Innovation from within* intends to do just that and to embed this same wonder into the context of nonprofits, so that with this spirit of curiosity we might be compelled to dream up solutions to the problems we are passionate about. The social issues we face as nonprofits are longstanding and difficult. We need change makers with the sharpest minds and with the best tools who are committed towards real transformative change. We hope this book is a contribution towards that.

This book is not meant to be read once and then put back on the shelf. We want this book to be read and reread, borrowed and shared, scanned and photocopied. We want this book and these concepts to breathe new life into the way we think and to permeate the way we work because we believe that by utilizing our creativity and all our existing resources, we will create real sustainable change in our communities—and nonprofits will be leading the way.

GLOSSARY

AFFILIATION A scaling method that involves creating a network of integrated programs that have to adhere to particular standards, principles, or practices to use the brand.

ALPHA PROTOTYPE A simple mock-up or descriptor of a model that allows feedback and refinement without a significant investment of resources. It can be a sketch, a written description, or a 3-D version of the solution using easy to obtain materials.

BEGINNER'S MINDSET A way to approach each situation as a new experience with an open mind, as if you were experiencing it for the first time.

BENEFIT CORPORATION (B-CORP) A type of for-profit entity that pursues social and/or environmental impact in addition to financial gain. Shareholders are required to consider the impact of decisions on society in addition to their responsibility to maximize profit.

BETA PROTOTYPE A small-scale, inexpensive, functional model of a proposed solution.

BIG DATA A term that describes large and complex datasets that require nontraditional processing methods and can be used to examine trends and patterns.

BRANCHING Developing local branches of a central organization.

CAUSE MARKETING Marketing efforts that pair for-profit businesses with nonprofit organizations/causes to raise money for the company and cause, and to increase awareness.

COMMONS CREATING Developing, nurturing, and growing shared assets.

COMMUNITY-LED PRACTICE A process that promotes the ability of the community to be the leader of its own interventions.

CORPORATE SOCIAL RESPONSIBILITY A self-regulated business model that supports initiatives or business practices to benefit society.

CROWDFUNDING Raising money from a large number of individuals, often making use of the Internet or social media.

CROWDSOURCING Enlisting a large number of people (paid or unpaid) to contribute solutions toward project tasks. Typically, contributions are derived from the Internet.

CULTURAL HUMILITY/CULTURAL SENSITIVITY The ability to understand things from the perspective of those you engage with, particularly as they relate to aspects of culture.

DESIGN THINKING A user-centered design process that uses overlapping phases to understand a problem, ideate and test solutions, and implement results.

DISSEMINATION Sharing ideas, tools, and resources to scale.

DOT VOTING A process of voting in which each team member is given three dots to distribute among various possible options.

EMPATHIC INQUIRY Investigation into a topic through asking questions, searching for knowledge, seeking insight, and getting deeper into a subject with the perspective that another holds the information rather than assuming the researcher already has all the information needed to act.

EMPATHY The ability to understand others in an authentic and reciprocal way.

EMPOWERMENT The degree of power and autonomy that people have to act on their own interests.

ENTREPRENEURSHIP The willingness and activity to develop, set up, and manage a business venture with the accompanying risk in order to make a profit. Broader conceptualizations include the activity of working creatively to solve problems and create value.

FEASIBLE Something that can be carried out given the current climate and resources.

FOURTH SECTOR Organizations that use an integrated approach that combines market and social/environmental approaches.

GAMIFICATION The application of game strategies or processes to achieve an educational or social goal.

GEOGRAPHIC INFORMATION SYSTEMS (GIS) A system that uses geographic or spatial data to map and understand relationships and patterns.

HACKATHON An event that brings multiple people together to do collaborative computer programming using a fast-paced approach. It has also been applied to other events used to develop solutions in a short period of time with a range of contributors.

IDEATION A creative process of iterative idea generation and development.

IMPACT INVESTING Investing in companies that create environmental or social benefit in addition to financial return.

INFORMATION AND COMMUNICATION TECHNOLOGY (ICT) An umbrella term for technologies used for communication and the integration of communication; it applies to the hardware as well as software and systems that allow users to transmit, store, and manipulate information.

INNOVATION A process, method, product, or outcome that is new and creates an improvement.

ITERATION The repetition of a process; used in design to refer to repetition that moves the process closer to achieving the desired result.

LOW-PROFIT LIMITED LIABILITY CORPORATION (L3C) A legal business entity in the United States with a social mission and profit as a secondary aim. It allows for program-related investments in for-profit organizations with social benefit.

LEADERSHIP DIFFUSION Decentralizing decision-making so that multiple people are able to weigh in on the direction an organization takes.

MOBILE TECHNOLOGY Technology made available through cellular phones.

NONPROFIT INNOVATION MODEL An innovation process designed to leverage existing resources and support nonprofits through innovation in their own environment.

OPEN INNOVATION The power and process to harness external ideas and approaches to further the mission of an organization by engaging with external sources.

POSITIVE DEVIANCE An approach to understanding phenomena by observing people who are successful despite facing similar challenges to their peers.

PROCESS INNOVATION A new approach to the way an organization operates that results in a more sustainable outcome.

RAPID PROTOTYPING A process of quick iteration to develop a model of a solution.

REPLICATION A scaling method to reproduce the same solution an additional time or in an additional location.

RIGHT-HANDED PATTERN BREAKING A concept that asks people to consider barriers to access of historically marginalized communities by reflecting on the overwhelming dominance of products for right-handed individuals and the barriers that such products create for left-handed people.

ROOT CAUSE The underlying cause of a phenomena that, if eliminated, would prevent the phenomena from occurring.

SCALING Bringing a product, program, initiative, or other solution to a larger beneficiary group so that it can have more significant impact.

SIMULATION The process of pretending, acting out, or imitating a situation to learn from the experience.

SOCIAL BUSINESS An organization that is profit-oriented and also has a clear social mission.

SOCIAL EMBEDDEDNESS A dual understanding of the word "social" as it pertains to both a social purpose and the social requirement for interaction.

SOCIAL ENTERPRISE The use of business models or practices to solve social problems. May refer to the socially driven organization or venture that uses market-oriented approaches to achieve its social mission. The revenue generated in a social enterprise is often reinvested into the social mission of the organization.

SOCIAL ENTREPRENEURSHIP The use of entrepreneurial principles (including risk-taking, innovative approaches, change orientation, sustainable business model) to develop a business or organization to respond to social issues. While social entrepreneurship has taken on a broader definition about transformative solutions to social problems, it is most typically portrayed as an individual or small group starting or forming something new.

SOCIAL FINANCE An investment strategy and funding source that simultaneously works to achieve financial gain and social benefit.

SOCIAL IMPACT ASSESSMENT An evaluation methodology to review the social impact of a solution.

SOCIAL IMPACT BOND A contract between the government, a social organization, and a private investor. The government agrees to pay the organization for services in exchange for improved social outcomes. Payment does not occur until a predetermined socially beneficial outcome is reached. Investors outside of government are brought in to fund these contracts.

SOCIAL INNOVATION An umbrella term that encompasses multiple pathways and processes that address the root causes of social injustices. The solutions are more effective, efficient, and/or sustainable—socially, economically, and environmentally—than previous solutions and are a result of collaboration with diverse stakeholders.

SOCIAL INTRAPRENEURSHIP The use of entrepreneurial principles within an existing organization or institution to solve social problems.

SOCIAL SECTOR Broad range of organizations that are primarily dedicated to social impact, responding to social and/or environmental issues. It includes nonprofits, charities, nongovernmental organizations, social enterprises, and social ventures.

SOCIAL VENTURE An organization (could be nonprofit, for-profit, or hybrid) that works to achieve social mission above financial gains.

SOCIAL VENTURE CAPITAL Type of investment typically using seed funding to invest in social enterprises to achieve financial gain and social impact.

STORYTELLING The use of narratives to inspire and share with others.

STRENGTHS-BASED PRACTICE A framework of thinking that utilizes the user's strengths as a starting point for working toward a solution.

SUSTAINABLE/SUSTAINABILITY Concerned with the long-term success of an initiative and considers the impact on people, profit, and the planet.

TRIANGULATION A tool that uses multiple data sources to cross-verify findings.

UNLIKELY SUSPECTS People who might not typically be involved in a specific project area.

VENTURE PHILANTHROPY Targeting resources (grants or investments) to a particular systemic issue with a longer period of investment and intensive engagement between the investor and recipient.

WEARABLE TECHNOLOGIES Smart electronic devices that can be worn to provide feedback, information, or tracking.

REFERENCES

Agocs, C. (1997). Institutional resistance to organizational change: Denial, inaction, and repression. *Journal of Business Ethics, 16,* 917–931.

Alexander, M. (2011). *The new Jim Crow.* New York: New Press.

Bendell, J. (2010). *Evolving partnerships: A guide to working with business for greater social change.* Sheffield, UK: Greenleaf.

Berzin, S. C., Pitt-Catsouphes, M., & Gaitan-Rossi, P. (2015). Defining our own future: Human service leaders on social innovation. *Human Service Organizations: Management, Leadership & Governance,* 1–14. doi: 10.1080/23303131.2015.1060914

Berzin, S. C., Pitt-Catsouphes, M., & Peterson, C. (2014). Role of state-level governments in fostering social innovation. *Journal of Policy Practice, 13*(3), 135–155.

Berzin, S. C., Singer, J., & Chan, C. (2015). *Practice innovation through technology in the digital age: A grand challenge for social work.* Grand Challenges for Social Work Initiative Working Paper No. 12. Cleveland, OH: American Academy of Social Work and Social Welfare.

Blackwood, A. S., Roeger, K. L., & Pettijohn, S. L. (2012). *The nonprofit sector in brief: Public charities, giving, and volunteering,* 2012. Washington, DC: Urban Institute.

Blumenthal, N. (2016). The secret to innovation at Warby Parker: Think like a beginner. https://www.linkedin.com/pulse/secret-innovation-warby-parker-think-like-beginner-neil-blumenthal

Boynton, A., & Fisher, B. (2005). *Virtuoso teams: Lessons from teams that changed their worlds.* Boston, MA: Prentice Hall Financial Times.

Brown, T. (2009). *Change by design: How design thinking transforms organizations and inspires innovation.* New York: Harper Collins.

Bureau of Labor Statistics. (2016). *Entrepreneurship and the US economy.*

Caldicott, S. M. (2012). *Midnight lunch: The 4 phases of team collaboration success from Thomas Edison's Lab.* Hoboken, NJ: John Wiley & Sons.

Chafkin, M. (2015). Warby Paker: For building the first great made-on-the-Internet brand. *Fast Company.*

Chell, E., Nicolopoulou, K., & Karatas-Ozkan, M. (2010). Social entrepreneurship and enterprise: International and innovation perspectives. *Entrepreneurship & Regional Development, 22*(6), 485–493.

Commongood Careers (Producer). (2016). Innovation@Work: Daily staff ritual keeps spirits high. http://commongoodcareers.org/blog/detail/daily-staff-ritual-keeps-spirits-high

Dacin, M. T., Dacin, P. A., & Tracey, P. (2011). Social entrepreneurship: A critique and future directions. *Organization Science, 22*(5), 1203–1213.

Damanpour, F. (1991). Organizational innovation: A meta-analysis of effects of determinants and moderators. *Academy of Management, 34,* 555–590.

Dart, R. (2004). Being business-like in a nonprofit organization. A grounded and inductive typology. *Nonprofit and Voluntary Sector Quarterly, 33*(2), 290–310.

De, B. E. (1999). *Six thinking hats.* Boston: Back Bay Books.

Dees, G., & Anderson, B. B. (2004). Scaling social impact. *Stanford Social Innovation Review,* Spring. https://ssir.org/articles/entry/scaling_social_impact

Drucker, P. (1954). *The practice of management.* New York: HarperCollins.

Fixsen, D., Blase, K., Naoom, S., & Duda, M. (2013). *Implementation drivers: Assessing best practices.* Chapel Hill, NC: National Implementation Science Network.

Gilley, A., Godek, M., & Giley, J. W. (2009). Change, resistance, and the organizational immune system. *SAM Advanced Management Journal,* Autumn, 4–10.

Giving USA is *Giving USA 2016: The Annual Report on Philanthropy for the Year 2015,* a publication of Giving USA Foundation, 2016, researched and written by the Indiana University Lilly Family School of Philanthropy. Available online at the Giving USA store.

GSMA. (2014). *The Mobile Economy 2014.* https://www.gsmaintelligence.com/research/?file=bb688b369d6 4cfd5b4e05a1ccfcbcb48&download

Hansen-Turton, T., & Torres, N. D. (Eds.). (2014). *Social innovation and impact in nonprofit leadership.* New York: Springer.

Hill, L. A., Brandeau, G., Truelove, E., & Lineback, K. (2015). The capabilities your organization needs to sustain innovation. Harvard Business Review, January, 2015.

Husch, B. (2011). *The fiscal survey of states.* Washington, DC: National Governors Association and the National Association of State Budget Officers.

Jaruzelski, B., Schwartz, K., & Staack, V. (2015). *The 2015 Global Innovation 1000: Innovation's New World Order*: Strategy& PWC. https://www.strategyand.pwc.com/media/file/The-2015-Global-Innovation-1000-Media-report.pdf

Johansen, B. (2009). *Leaders make the future: Ten new leadership skills for an uncertain world.* San Francisco, CA: Berrett-Koehler.

Johnson, N., Oliff, P., & Williams, E. (2011). *An update on state budget cuts.* Washington, DC: Center on Budget and Policy Priorities.

Kotter, J. P. (1996). *Leading change.* Boston, MA: Harvard Business School Press.

Krishna, A. (2011). Can supporting a cause decrease donations and happiness? The cause marketing paradox. *Journal of Consumer Psychology, 21*(3), 338–345. doi: 10.1016/j.jcps.2011.02.001

Lawrence, S., & Mukai, R. (2011). *Foundation growth and giving estimates.* Foundation Center. http://foundationcenter.issuelab.org/resource/foundations-today-growth-and-giving-estimates-2011-edition.html

Light, P. C. (2008). *The search for social entrepreneurship.* Washington, DC: Brookings Institution Press.

Marshmallow Challenge. (2014). Home page. http://marshmallowchallenge.com/

Massolution. (2013). *The crowdfunding industry report.* Selangor, Malaysia.

Miller Caldicott, S. (2012). *Midnight Lunch: The 4 Phases of Team Collaboration Success from Thomas Edison's Lab.* Hoboken, NJ: Wiley.

Moore, M., & Westley, F. (2009). *Surmountable chasms: The role of cross-scale interactions in social innovation.* Social Innovation Generation. Waterloo, ONT: University of Waterloo.

Murray, R., Caulie-Grice, J., & Mulgan, G. (2010). *The open book of social innovation.* London: NESTA and the Young Foundation.

Nonprofit Finance Fund. (2014). *State of the nonprofit sector survey*. New York City. http://www.nonprofitfinancefund.org/sites/default/files/paragraphs/file/download/2014survey_brochure.pdf

Osterwalder, A. (2015). The C-suite needs a chief entrepreneur. *Harvard Business Review*, June. https://hbr.org/2015/06/the-c-suite-needs-a-chief-entrepreneur

Osterwalder, A., & Pigneur, Y. (2010). *Business model generation: A handbook for visionaries, game changers, and challengers*. Hoboken, NJ: Wiley.

Pallotta, D. (2008). *Uncharitable: How restraints on nonprofits undermine their potential*. Lebanon, NH: Tufts University Press.

Pallotta, D. (2013). The way we think about charity is dead wrong. Video file. https://www.ted.com/talks/dan_pallotta_the_way_we_think_about_charity_is_dead_wrong/transcript?language=en

Pettijohn, S. L. (2013). *The nonprofit sector in brief: Public charities, giving, and volunteering*, 2013. Washington, DC: Urban Institute.

Phills, J. A., Deiglmeier, K., & Miller, D. T. (2008). Rediscovering social innovation. *Stanford Social Innovation Review, 6*(4), 34–43.

Pinchot, G., & Pellman, R. (1999). *Intrapreneuring in action: A handbook for business innovation*. San Francisco, CA: Berrett-Koehler.

Pitt-Catsouphes, M., & Berzin, S. C. (2015). Incorporating social innovation content in macro social work education. *Journal of Social Work Education, 51*, 407–416.

Pitt-Catsouphes, M., de Zengotita, L., & Berzin, S. C. (2013). *Leading the way: Social innovation in Massachusetts*. Boston, MA: Providers' Council.

Roeger, K. L., Blackwood, A. S., & Pettijohn, S. L. (2012). *The nonprofit almanac*. Washington, DC: Urban Institute Press.

Rüedel, D., & Lurtz, K. (2012). *Mapping the various meanings of social innovation: Towards a differentiated understanding of an emerging concept*. Oestrich-Winkel, GER: EBS Business School Research Paper Series.

Sabeti, H., & Fourth Sector Network Concept Working Group. (2009). *The emerging fourth sector*. Washington, DC: Aspen Institute.

Sage, M. (2014). Use of Web 2.0 to train facilitators in fidelity: A case study. *Journal of Technology in Human Services, 32*(1–2), 108–118. doi: 10.1080/15228835.2014.886982

Salamon, L. M., Sokolowski, S. W., & Geller, S. L. (2012). *Holding the fort: Nonprofit employment during a decade of turmoil*. Baltimore, MD: Center for Civil Society Studies.

Singer, S., Amorós, J. E., & Moska, D. (2015). *Global entrepreneurship monitor*. London: Global Entrepreneurship Research Association.

Stevenson, H. H. (1983). *A perspective on entrepreneurship*. Cambridge, MA: Harvard Business School Press.

Suzuki, S. (2006). *Zen mind, beginner's mind*. Boston, MA: Shambhala.

Tushman, M., & Nadler, D. (1986). Organizing for innovation. *California Management Review, 28*(3), 74–92.

Van de Ven, A. H., & Sun, K. S. (2011). Breakdowns in implementing models of organization change. *Academy of Management Perspectives, 25*, 58–74.

Waddell, C. (2001). So much research evidence, so little dissemination and uptake: Mixing the useful with the pleasing. *Evidence Based Mental Health, 4*, 3–5. doi: 10.1136/ebmh.4.1.3

Wing, K., Roeger, K. L., & Pollack, T. H. (2010). *The nonprofit sector in brief: Public charities, giving, and volunteering, 2010*. Washington, DC: Urban Institute.

The Young Foundation. (2012). *Social innovation overview: A deliverable of the project: The theoretical, empirical and policy foundations for building social innovation in Europe (TEPSIE)*. Brussels: European Commission 7th Framework Programme: European Commission, DG Research.

INDEX

CPSIA information can be obtained
at www.ICGtesting.com
Printed in the USA
BVHW061552180921
616968BV00004B/15